BY FRANK BIDART

Golden State

The Book of the Body

The Sacrifice

In the Western Night—Collected Poems 1965–90

In the Western Night

Collected Poems 1965-90

IN THE

WESTERN

NIGHT

Collected Poems 1965-90

Frank Bidart

Farrar Straus Giroux

New York

Library of Congress Cataloging-in-Publication Data
Bidart, Frank
In the western night—collected poems 1965–90 / Frank Bidart.—
1st ed.
I. Title.
PS3552.I33I5   1990   811'.54—dc20   89-25993

Acknowledgment is made to the following for permission to reprint
previously published material: Basic Books for permission to reprint
excerpts from Ludwig Binswanger's Der Fall Ellen West, translated by
Werner M. Mendel and Joseph Lyons, included in Existence, edited by
Rollo May, Ernest Angel, and Henri F. Ellenberger, © 1958 by Basic
Books, Inc., Publishers, New York. / Columbia University Press for
permission to reprint phrases from Wilhelm Dilthey's "The Dream," in
Wilhelm Dilthey's Philosophy of History by William Kluback,
© 1956 by Columbia University Press. Used by permission. / Simon &
Schuster for permission to reprint excerpts from Nijinsky by Romola
Nijinsky, copyright 1934, © 1961 by Romola Nijinsky. Reprinted by
permission of Simon & Schuster. All other rights controlled by Eric
Glass Ltd, London. Acknowledgment is also made to the following where
previously uncollected work first appeared: The Agni Review, Antaeus,
The New Republic, The New York Review of Books,
Ploughshares, The Threepenny Review.

ISBN 0-374-52271-5

Contents

Golden State (1973)

The First Hour of the Night (1990)

Appendix

In the Western Night

(1990)

To the Dead

What I hope (when I hope) is that we'll
see each other again,—

. . . and again reach the VEIN

in which we loved each other . . .
It existed. *It existed.*

There is a NIGHT within the NIGHT,—

. . . for, like the detectives (the Ritz Brothers)
in *The Gorilla*,

once we'd been battered by the gorilla

we searched the walls, the intricately carved
impenetrable panelling

for a button, lever, latch

that unlocks a secret door that
reveals at last the secret chambers,

CORRIDORS within WALLS,

(the disenthralling, necessary, dreamed structure
beneath the structure we see,)

that is the HOUSE within the HOUSE . . .

There is a NIGHT within the NIGHT,—

. . . there were (for example) months when I seemed only
to displease, frustrate,

disappoint you—; then, something triggered

a drunk lasting for days, and as you
slowly and shakily sobered up,

sick, throbbing with remorse and self-loathing,

insight like ashes: clung
to; useless; hated . . .

This was the viewing of the power of the waters

while the waters were asleep:—
secrets, histories of loves, betrayals, double-binds

not fit (you thought) for the light of day . . .

There is a NIGHT within the NIGHT,—

. . . for, there at times at night, still we
inhabit the secret place together . . .

Is this wisdom, or self-pity?—

The love I've known is the love of
two people staring

not at each other, but in the same direction.

Dark Night

(John of the Cross)

In a dark night, when the light
    burning was the burning of love (*fortuitous*
    night, fated, free, —)
    as I stole from my dark house, dark
    house that was silent, grave, sleeping, —

by the staircase that was secret, hidden,
    safe: disguised by darkness (*fortuitous*
    night, fated, free, —)
    by darkness and by cunning, dark
    house that was silent, grave, sleeping—;

in that sweet night, secret, seen by
    no one and seeing
    nothing, my only light or
    guide
    the burning in my burning heart,

night was the guide
    to the place where he for whom I
    waited, whom I had long ago chosen,
    waits: night
    brighter than noon, in which none can see—;

night was the guide
    sweeter than the sun raw at
    dawn, for there the burning bridegroom is
    bride
    and he who chose at last is chosen.

As he lay sleeping on my sleepless
    breast, kept from the beginning for him
    alone, lying on the gift I gave
    as the restless
    fragrant cedars moved the restless winds,—

winds from the circling parapet circling
    us as I lay there touching and lifting his hair,—
    with his sovereign hand, he
    wounded my neck—
    and my senses, when they touched that, touched nothing . . .

In a dark night (*there where I*
    lost myself, —) as I leaned to rest
    in his smooth white breast, everything
    ceased
    and left me, forgotten in the grave of forgotten lilies.

In the Western Night

1. The Irreparable

First, I was there where unheard
harmonies create the harmonies

we hear —

then I was a dog, sniffing
your crotch.

I asked you why you
were here; your answer was your beauty.

I said I was in need. You said
that the dead

rule and confuse our steps —

that if I helped you cut your skin
deeply enough

that, at least, was IRREPARABLE . . .

This afternoon, the clouds
were moving so swiftly —

massed above the towers, rushing.

2. In My Desk

Two cigarette butts—
left by you

the first time you visited my apartment.
The next day

I found them, they were still there—

picking one up, I put my lips where
yours had been . . .

       ·

Our not-love is like a man running down
a mountain, who, if he dares to try to stop,

falls over—
my hands wanted to touch your hands

because we had hands.

       ·

I put the two cigarette butts
in an envelope, carefully

taping shut the edges.
At first, the thin paper of the envelope

didn't stop

the stale smell of tobacco . . .
Now the envelope is in my desk.

3. Two Men

The man who does not know himself, who
does not know his affections that his actions

speak but that he does not
acknowledge,

who will SAY ANYTHING

and lie when he does not know that he is
lying because what he needs to believe is true

must indeed
be true,

THIS MAN IS STONE . . . NOT BREAD.

STONE. NOT CAKE. NOT CHEESE. NOT BREAD . . .

The man who tries to feed his hunger
by gnawing stone

is a FOOL; his hunger is

fed in ways that he knows cannot satisfy it.

4. Epilogue: A Stanza from Horace

At night in dreams I hold you
    and now I pursue you
fleeing through the grass of the Campus Martius,
you, through the waters (you are cruel) fleeing.

Berkeley, California; 1983.

Poem in the Stanza of the "Rubaiyat"

1. Spirit

The present and the future are the past
Now that her body cannot wake, nor, lost
    Between the kitchen and the wilderness,
Rest—haunted by ghosts, now become a ghost.

2. Reading the "Rubaiyat"

Because she loved it even as a girl,
She taught her child to love it—as he still
    Does, hearing as he reads beneath his voice
Her voice . . . past Waste, the gorgeous, trickling Well.

3. Christmas Eve in Harvard Square

Child, when you learn that the laughing ghosts who live
Shadowing your steps in forty years give
    Substancelessness to stone, is this night one
More thing you'll try to kill in you to live?

In the Ruins

1. *Man is a MORAL animal.*

2. *You can get human beings to do anything,—IF
   you convince them it is moral.*

3. *You can convince human beings anything is moral.*

      •   •   •

Oh Night,—

    . . . THE SUN IS DEAD.

                    What we dream moves
across our sky by

day, is a CORPSE,—

that sun's day is not the *real* day—;
that day's light is not the *real* light—;

FOR THE SUN IS DEAD . . .

            Now when I learned this,

I knew the injunction placed upon me.
Before the corpse, I heard:—

        RETURN THE DEAD TO LIFE.

Guilty of Dust

up or down from the infinite C E N T E R
B R I M M I N G at the winking rim of time

the voice in my head said

LOVE IS THE DISTANCE
BETWEEN YOU AND WHAT YOU LOVE

WHAT YOU LOVE IS YOUR FATE

.

then I saw the parade of my loves

those PERFORMERS comics actors singers

forgetful of my very self so often I
desired to die to myself to live in them

then my PARENTS my FRIENDS the drained
SPECTRES once filled with my baffled infatuations

love and guilt and fury and
sweetness for whom

nail spirit yearning to the earth

.

then the voice in my head said

WHETHER YOU LOVE WHAT YOU LOVE

OR LIVE IN DIVIDED CEASELESS
REVOLT AGAINST IT

WHAT YOU LOVE IS YOUR FATE

1984.

The Sacrifice

(1983)

. . . the speculative Good Friday in place of the historic Good Friday. Good Friday must be speculatively re-established in the whole truth and harshness of its Godforsakenness.

—HEGEL

The War of Vaslav Nijinsky

Still gripped by the illusion of an horizon;
overcome with the finality of a broken tooth;
suspecting that habits are the only salvation,

—the Nineteenth Century's
guilt, *World War One,*

was danced

by Nijinsky on January 19, 1919.

        •   •   •

. . . I am now reading *Ecce Homo.* Nietzsche
is *angry* with me—;

he hates "the Crucified One."

But he did not live through War—;
when the whole world painted its face

with blood.

Someone must expiate the blood.

        •   •   •

No. Let what is past
be forgotten. Let even the blood

be forgotten—; there *can be no* "expiation."

Expiation is not necessary.

Suffering has made me what I am,—

I must not regret; or judge; or
struggle to escape it

in the indifference of (the ruthless
ecstasy of)
        CHANGE; "my endless RENEWAL"; BECOMING.

—That is Nietzsche.

He wants to say *"Yes"* to life.

I am not Nietzsche. I am the bride of Christ.

    •   •   •

He was planning a new and original ballet. It was to be a picture
of sex life, with the scene laid in a *maison tolérée.* The chief character
was to be the owner—once a beautiful *cocotte,* now aged and para-
lyzed as a result of her debauchery; but, though her body is a wreck,
her spirit is indomitable in the traffic of love. She deals with all the
wares of love, selling girls to boys, youth to age, woman to woman,
man to man.

    When he danced it, he succeeded in transmitting the whole
scale of sex life.

    •   •   •

—Many times Diaghilev wanted me
to make love to him

as if he were
a woman—;

I did. I *refuse* to
regret it.

      At first, I felt humiliated for him,—

he saw this. He got angry
and said, "I enjoy it!"

Then, more calmly, he said,

"Vatza, we must not *regret* what we *feel.*"

—I REGRETTED

        what I FELT . . . Not

making love, but that since the beginning
I wanted to *leave* him . . .
           That I stayed

out of "GRATITUDE,"—
         and *FEAR OF LIFE,*—
                and AMBITION . . .

That in my soul,
        I did *not* love him.

Now my wife wants to have
a second child. I am frightened;

the things a human being must learn,—
the things a child

must *learn* he FEELS,—

frighten me! I know people's faults

because in my soul,
        I HAVE COMMITTED THEM.

The man who chops wood for us
was speaking, this morning, in the kitchen,

to my wife. As I passed in the hallway
I heard

whispering—; and LISTENED . . .

He said that as a child
in his village at Sils Maria

he worked for the writer, *Nietzsche*—;
he felt he must tell her

that just before the "famous man"
was taken away, INSANE,

he acted and looked

AS I DO NOW.

I can choose *"life"* for myself;—

but must I, again, again,
AGAIN,—
        for *any other* creature?

·   ·   ·

The Durcals arrived in St. Moritz, and were invited to tea. Asked
what he had been doing lately, Vaslav put on a worldly air, leaned
back on the sofa and said,
    "Well, I composed two ballets, I prepared a new program for
the next Paris season, and lately—I have played a part. You see, I
am an artist; I have no troupe now, so I miss the stage. I thought
it would be rather an interesting experiment to see how well I could
act, and so for six weeks I played the part of a lunatic; and the whole

village, my family, and even the physicians apparently believed it. I have a male nurse to watch me, in the disguise of a *masseur.*"

Romola was overcome, torn between anger and relief. She was confirmed in her supposition that her fears had been groundless when the male nurse came, after ten days, to assure her from his long experience that her husband was completely sane.

·　　　·　　　·

—Let me explain to you
what *"guilt"* is . . .

When I joke with my wife, and say,
"I think I will go back to Russia
and live as a peasant—"

she jokes back, and says,
"Do as you like! I will
divorce you, and marry
　　　　　　　　a manufacturer . . ."

She looks at me, and I look at her.

What is terrible

is that I am serious—; and *she* is serious . . .

She is right, of course,—
　　　　　　　　I do *not* have the right

to make her live differently, without servants,
rich friends, elegant clothes—
without her good and sane *habits*;

do not have the right even to try
to *re-make* her . . .

But does *she* then have the right
to make *me* live like this, JUDGED, surrounded by
those who cannot understand or *feel* me,—

                                         like a manufacturer? . . .

She is angry, as I am angry.

We both are *right*—; and both angry . . .

Soon, she feels guilty, feels that she
has failed me—;
                   and I too
feel guilty . . .

The *GUILT* comes from *NOWHERE*.

Neither of us has done wrong!

But I am a good actor—and reassure her
that I love her; am indeed happy; and that
nothing will change . . .

I *want* to be a *good husband*.

Still, I am guilty.

                       . . . Why am I guilty?

My life is *FALSE*.

                •   •   •

I know the psychology of lunatics;
if you don't contradict them, they like you.

But I am not insane.

My brother was insane. He died
in a lunatic asylum.

The reason I *know* I am *NOT* insane
is because, unlike my brother,

I *feel guilt.*

The insane do not feel guilt.

My brother was a dancer. He was older than I,
but still in the *corps* when I became
a soloist. He was ashamed, and jealous;

he went insane.

When the doctors questioned him, he showed
astonishing courage,—
                              he thought that everyone
in the company was paid

by the secret police, to gather
evidence against our family . . .

He displayed cunning, and stoic
fortitude, under the questions.

Even when he thought he faced death,
he lied
to protect my mother.

When he was taken away,
she cried, and cried . . .
                              She cried
visiting him,—

but that didn't make him feel GUILTY . . .

My wife thought because
I wore a large *cross* on my neck in the village,—

and told her certain dishes
served at our table were poisoned,—

I was insane.

But I *knew* that my actions
frightened her—; and I suffered.

Nietzsche was insane. He knew
we killed God.

        . . . This is the *end* of the story:

though He was dead, God was clever
and strong. God struck back,—

AND KILLED US.

If I *act* insane, people will call me
"mad clown," and forgive
                 even the truth—;

the insane feel anxiety and horror,

but are RELEASED
from GUILT . . .

I only want to know
things I've learned like this,—

these things I cannot *NOT* know.

            •   •   •

His other ballet remained unfinished. It was his own life put into
a choreographic poem: a youth seeking truth through life, first as a
pupil, open to all artistic suggestions, to all the beauty that life and

love can offer; then his love for the woman, his mate, who success-
fully carries him off.

He set it in the period of the High Renaissance. The youth is
a painter; his Master one of the greatest artists of the period, part
Genius and part Politician, just as Diaghilev seemed to him to be.
This Master advances him, and defends his daring work from the
attacks of colleagues, as long as he is a student; then he falls in love,
and the Master bitterly rejects not only him but his work.

•   •   •

—Last night, once again, I nearly
abandoned my autobiographical ballet . . .

The plot has a good beginning
and middle,—
                    THE PUZZLE

is the end . . .

The *nights* I spend—

                    reading and improving
Nietzsche, analyzing and then abandoning

my life, working on the *Great Questions*

like WAR and GUILT and GOD
and MADNESS,—

I rise from my books, my endless, fascinating
researches, notations, projects,

dazzled.
          —Is this happiness? . . .

I have invented a far more
accurate and specific notation for dance;

it has taken me two months
to write down the movement in my ten-minute

ballet, *L'Après-midi d'un Faune* . . .

There is a MORAL here

about how LONG you must live with
the consequences of a SHORT action,—

but I don't now feel
MORAL.
        Soon I shall begin

Le Sacre du Printemps — ; which
is longer . . .

I can understand the pleasures of War.

In War—
        where *killing* is a virtue: *camouflage*
a virtue: *revenge* a virtue:
pity a weakness—
        the world rediscovers

a *guiltless* PRE-HISTORY

"civilization" condemns . . .

In 1914, I was assured
the War would end in six weeks;

the Germans, in the summer, thought
they would enter Paris by the fall.

But the War
        was *NOT* an accident.

CUSTOM, and his Children,—

Glory. Honor. Privilege. Poverty.
Optimism. "The Balance of Power,"—

for four years

dug a large, long hole
(—a *TRENCH*—)
                        in the earth of Europe;

when they approached the hole
to pin medals

on the puppets
they had thrown there,

they slipped in BLOOD,—

. . . AND FELL IN.

Poverty and *Privilege*
alone survived,

of all the customs of the past . . .

—Should the World
regret the War? Should I

REGRET MY LIFE?

. . . Let our epitaph be:

In Suffering, and Nightmare,
I woke at last

to my own nature.

•   •   •

One Sunday we decided to sleigh over to Maloja.

Kyra was glad and Vaslav was very joyful that morning.

It took us about three hours to get there; Kyra and I got very hungry during the long drive.

The road was extremely narrow during the winter, because it needed cleaning from the heavy snows, and in certain parts there was always a space to await the sleighs coming from the opposite direction.

Vaslav was as a rule a careful and excellent driver, but on this particular Sunday he did not wait, but simply *drove on into* the oncoming sleighs.

We were in danger of turning over; the horses got frightened.

The coachmen of the other sleighs cursed, but this did not make any difference.

Kyra screamed, and I begged Vaslav to be more careful, but the further we went the more fiercely he drove *against* the other sleighs.

I had to clutch on to Kyra and the sleigh to keep ourselves on.

I was furious, and said so to Vaslav.

He fixed me suddenly with a hard and metallic look which I had never seen before.

As we arrived at the Maloja Inn I ordered a meal.

We had to wait.

Vaslav asked for some bread and butter and macaroni.

"Ah, Tolstoy again," I thought, but did not say a word, and bit my lips.

Kyra was anxiously awaiting her steak, and as it was laid before her and she began to eat, Vaslav, with a quick gesture, snatched the plate away.

She began to cry from disappointment.

I exclaimed, "Now, Vaslav, please don't begin that Tolstoy nonsense again; you remember how weak you got by starving yourself on that vegetarian food. I can't stop you doing it, but I won't allow you to interfere with Kyra. The child must eat properly."

I went with Kyra to the other room to have our solitary lunch.

We drove home very quietly without a word.

·   ·   ·

—The second part of my ballet
Le Sacre du Printemps

                    is called "THE SACRIFICE."

A young girl, a virgin, is chosen
to die
so that the Spring will return,—

so that her Tribe (free
from *"pity," "introspection," "remorse"*)

out of her blood
can renew itself.

The fact that the earth's renewal
requires human blood

is unquestioned; a mystery.

She is chosen, from the whirling, stamping
circle of her peers, purely by chance—;

then, driven from the circle, surrounded
by the elders, by her peers, by animal
skulls impaled on pikes,

she dances,—

            at first, in paroxysms
of Grief, and Fear:—

                    again and again, she leaps (—*NOT*

as a ballerina leaps, as if she
loved the air, as if
the air were her element—)

SHE LEAPS

BECAUSE SHE HATES THE GROUND.

But then, slowly, as others
join in, she finds that there is a self

WITHIN herself

that is *NOT* HERSELF

impelling her to accept,—and at last
to *LEAD*,—

        THE DANCE

that is her own sacrifice . . .

—In the end, exhausted, she falls
to the ground . . .

She dies; and her last breath
is the reawakened Earth's

orgasm,—
        a little upward run on the flutes
mimicking

        (—or perhaps MOCKING—)

the god's spilling
seed . . .

The Chosen Virgin
accepts her fate: without considering it,

she knows that her Tribe,—
the Earth itself,—
        are UNREMORSEFUL

that the price of continuance
is her BLOOD:—

                 she *accepts* their guilt,—

. . . THEIR GUILT

THAT THEY DO NOT KNOW EXISTS.

She has become, to use
our term,
              a *Saint*.

The dancer I chose for this role
detested it.

She would have preferred to do
a fandango, with a rose in her teeth . . .

The training she and I shared,—

training in the traditional
                 "academic" dance,—

emphasizes the illusion
                 of *Effortlessness,*
Ease, Smoothness, Equilibrium . . .

When I look into my life,
these are not the qualities
                 I find there.

Diaghilev, almost alone
in the Diaghilev Ballet, UNDERSTOOD;

though he is not now, after my marriage
and *"betrayal,"*

INTERESTED in my choreographic ambitions . . .

Nevertheless, to fill a theatre,
he can be persuaded

to *hire* me as a dancer . . .

Last night I dreamt

I was slowly climbing
a long flight of steps.

Then I saw Diaghilev
and my wife

arm in arm
climbing the steps behind me . . .

I began to hurry, so that
they would not see me.

Though I climbed
as fast as I could, the space

between us
NARROWED . . .

Soon, they were a few feet behind me,—
I could hear them laughing,

gossiping, discussing CONTRACTS
and LAWSUITS . . .

They understood each other perfectly.

I stopped.

But they

DIDN'T STOP . . .

They climbed right past me,—
laughing, chatting,

NOT SEEING ME AT ALL . . .

—I should have been happy;

yet . . .
       wasn't.

I watched their backs,
as they happily

disappeared, climbing
up, out of my sight . . .

       •   •   •

Our days passed in continuous social activity.

Then one Thursday, the day when the governess and maid had their day off, I was making ready to take Kyra out for a walk when suddenly Vaslav came out of his room and looked at me very angrily.

"How dare you make such a noise? I can't work."

I looked up, surprised.

His face, his manner were strange; he had never spoken to me like this.

"I am sorry. I did not realize we were so loud."

Vaslav got hold of me then by my shoulders and shook me violently.

I clasped Kyra in my arms very close, then with one powerful movement Vaslav pushed me down the stairs.

I lost my balance, and fell with the child, who began to scream.

At the bottom, I got up, more astounded than terrified.

What was the matter with him?

He was still standing there menacingly.

I turned round, exclaiming, "You ought to be ashamed! You are behaving like a drunken *peasant.*"

A very changed Vaslav we found when we came home, docile and kind as ever.

I did not speak about the incident, either to him or to anybody else.

Then one day we went on an excursion and Vaslav again wore his cross over his sweater.

On our way home, he suddenly began to drive fiercely and the sleigh turned over.

Amazingly, no one was hurt.

I got really angry, and walked home with Kyra.

Of course, he was home ahead of us.

When I entered the house, the servant who worshipped Vaslav opened the door and said, "Madame, I think Monsieur Nijinsky is ill, or perhaps very drunk, for he acts so queerly. His voice is hoarse and his eyes all hazy. I am frightened."

I went to our bedroom.

Vaslav lay fully dressed on the bed, with the cross on, his eyes closed.

He seemed to be asleep.

I turned cautiously towards the door, and then noticed that heavy tears were streaming down his face.

"Vatza, how are you feeling? Are you angry with me?"

"It is nothing; let me sleep; I am tired."

•   •   •

Each night now I pray,
                    Let this cup

pass from me! . . .

But it is not a cup. It is my life.

I have *LEARNED*

　　　my *NATURE* . . .

I am insane,—
. . . or evil.

Today I walked out into the snow.

I said to myself:

　　　THREE TIMES
YOU TRIED TO HARM YOUR WIFE AND CHILD.

I said:

　　　LIE DOWN IN THE SNOW
AND DIE. YOU ARE EVIL.

I lay down in the snow . . .

I tried to go to sleep.
My HANDS

began to get cold, to FREEZE.

I was lying there a long, long time.
I did not feel cold any more . . .

Then, God said to me:

　　　GO HOME
AND TELL YOUR WIFE YOU ARE INSANE.

I said:

　　　Thank you, thank you, God!
I am not evil. I am insane.

I got up. I wanted to go home,—
and tell this news

to my wife.

Then, I said to God:

I am insane,—
my wife will suffer. I am guilty.

Forgive me for being insane.

God said:

GOD MADE YOU. GOD DOES NOT CARE
IF YOU ARE "GUILTY" OR NOT.

I said:

I CARE IF I AM GUILTY!

I CARE IF I AM GUILTY! . . .

God was silent.

Everything was SILENT.

I lay back down in the snow.

I wanted again to go to sleep, and die . . .

But my BODY did not want to die.
My BODY spoke to me:

There is no answer to your life.
You are insane; or evil.

There is only one thing that you can do:—

You must join YOUR GUILT

to the WORLD'S GUILT.

I said to myself:

I must join MY GUILT

to the WORLD'S GUILT.

I got up out of the snow.
. . . What did the words mean?

Then I realized what the words meant.

I said to myself:

You must join YOUR GUILT

to the WORLD'S GUILT.

There is no answer to your life.
You are insane; or evil.

. . . Let this be the Body

through which the War has passed.

. . .

Nijinsky invited guests to a recital at the Suvretta House Hotel.
    When the audience was seated, he picked up a chair, sat down on it, and stared at them. Half an hour passed. Then he took a few rolls of black and white velvet and made a big cross the length of the room. He stood at the head of it, his arms opened wide. He said: "Now, I will dance you the War, which you did not prevent and for which you are responsible." His dance reflected battle, horror, catastrophe, apocalypse. An observer wrote: "At the end, we were

too much overwhelmed to applaud. We were looking at a corpse, and our silence was the silence that enfolds the dead."

There was a collection for the Red Cross. Tea was served. Nijinsky never again performed in public.

·   ·   ·

—The War is a *good* subject . . .

The audience, yesterday, liked
my dance.

The public does not understand *Art*;
it wants to be astonished.

I know how to astonish.

The War allowed me
to project,—
            to EMBODY,—

an ultimate *"aspect"* of the *"self"* . . .   ˈ

A member of the audience told me
I had always been able

"to smell a good subject."

God, on the other hand,—

                    who at times
has responded to my predilection

for *ACTIONS*

that are *METAPHYSICAL EXPERIMENTS*,—

perhaps felt threatened, or even
coerced—;

42

he perhaps felt that though he could
agree with me

that expiation *IS* necessary,—

he had to agree with
Nietzsche

that expiation is *NOT* possible . . .

In any case, he has chosen,—as
so often,—
                    CAMOUFLAGE . . .

Now that the War has been over
two months, at times I almost
doubt if it existed—;

in truth,
          it never existed,—

. . . *BECAUSE IT HAS NEVER BEEN OVER.*

Twenty years ago, a boy of nine
was taken by his mother

to the Imperial School of Ballet,

to attempt to become a pupil;

the mother was poor, and
afraid of life; his father

had abandoned the family when the boy was four . . .

Even then, he had a good jump—;
he was admitted.

He had been taught by the priests
that because of Adam and Eve, all men were born
in *Original Sin*,—

                that all men were,
BY NATURE, guilty . . .

In his soul, he didn't believe it.

He was a good boy. His mother loved him.

He believed
in his essential innocence,—

he thought his nature
                GOOD . . .

He worked hard. He grew thinner,—
and started

        "dancing like God" . . .

Everyone talked about it.

But then,—
        he LEARNED SOMETHING.

He learned that

        All life exists

at the expense of other life . . .

When he began to succeed,
he saw that he was AMBITIOUS,—
                    JEALOUS
of the roles that others won . . .

—Then his brother
got sick . . .

THE ROCK
           THAT GIVES SHADE TO ONE CREATURE,—

FOR ANOTHER CREATURE

                  JUST BLOCKS THE SUN.

. . . This is a problem of *BEING*.
                I can imagine

no *SOLUTION* to this . . .

At sixteen, he met a Prince. He loved the Prince,—
but after a time

the Prince grew tired of him . . .

Then he met a Count—;
             whom he *didn't* love.

The Count gave him a piano . . .

He had heard of Diaghilev. Diaghilev
invited him
        to the *Hotel Europe,*—

he went to seek his luck.

He found
his luck.

At once, he allowed Diaghilev
to make love to him.

Even then, he disliked Diaghilev
for his too self-assured voice . . .

He always had thought he was essentially
different from the people
                    in books of HISTORY,—

with their lives of *betrayals*; *blindness*;
greed; and *miseries* . . .

He saw, one day, that this illusion,—
this FAITH,—

                    had, imperceptibly,

vanished—;

                    he was *NOT* different—;

he did not understand *WHY* he did
what he did, nor were his instincts

"GOOD" . . .

Then, I said to myself:

                    "HISTORY *IS* HUMAN NATURE—;

TO SAY *I AM GUILTY*
                    IS TO ACCEPT IMPLICATION

IN THE HUMAN RACE . . ."

—Now, for months and months,
I have found

ANOTHER MAN in me—;

HE is NOT me—; I

am afraid of him . . .

He hates my wife and child,—
and hates Diaghilev;

because he thinks GOODNESS and BEING
are incompatible,—

. . . HE WANTS TO DESTROY THE WORLD.

DESTROY it,—
                    or REDEEM it.

Are they the *same?* . . .

As a child, I was taught, by the priests,
to crave the Last Judgment:—

when the *Earth* will become a *Stage,*—

and WHAT IS RIGHT and WHAT IS WRONG

will at last show *clear,* and *distinct,*
and *separate,*—

and then,—

                    THE SLATE IS WIPED CLEAN . . .

—Even now, I can see the World
wheeling on its axis . . . I

shout at it:—

                    CEASE. CHANGE,—
                              OR CEASE.

The World says right back:—

*I must chop down the Tree of Life
to make coffins . . .*

Tomorrow, I will go to Zurich—
to live in an asylum.

MY SOUL IS SICK,—
                    NOT MY MIND.

I *am* incurable . . . I did not
live long.

Death came
unexpectedly,—
                    for I wanted it to come.

Romola. Diaghilev.

. . . I HAVE EATEN THE WORLD.

My life is the expiation for my life.

Nietzsche understood me.

When *he* was sick,—when his *SOUL*
was sick,—
                    he wrote that he would have

much preferred to be a *Professor* at Basel

than *God*—;
                    but that he did not dare to carry

his egotism
so far as to neglect the Creation of the World.

In 1923, Diaghilev came to see him. Vaslav by now got out of bed in a strange fashion. First of all he went on all-fours; then crawled around the room; and only then stood upright. In a general way, he seemed attracted by the floor, to feel a need to be as low down as possible (his bed was almost on a level with the floor) and to grab hold of something. As he walked he leaned forward and felt at his ease only when lying down.

This was the first time Diaghilev had set eyes on him since they had parted in wrath in Barcelona six years before. "Vatza, you are being lazy. Come, I need you. You must dance again for the Russian Ballet and for me."

Vaslav shook his head. "I cannot because I am mad."

•　　　•　　　•

Frightened to eat with a new set of teeth;
exhausted by the courage the insane have shown;
uncertain whether to REDEEM or to DESTROY THE EARTH,

—the Nineteenth Century's
guilt, *World War One*,

was danced

by Nijinsky on January 19, 1919.

For Mary Ann Youngren

1932–1980

Mary Ann, as they handed you the cup
near the black waters of Lethe,

(the cup of *Forgetfulness,*
the waters of *Obliteration,*)

did you reach for it greedily—

just as, alive, you abruptly needed

not to answer the phone for days: ballet tickets
unused: awake all night: pacing

the apartment: untouchable: chain-smoking?

Dip a finger into the River of Time,—
it comes back
        STAINED.

        •

No, that's *not* enough,—
not true, wrong—

dying of cancer, eager to have the whole thing
over, you nonetheless waited

for your sister to arrive from California
before you died,—

you needed to bring up your cruelest, worst
adolescent brutality, asking:

DO YOU FORGIVE ME?

Then: WILL YOU MISS ME?

At the Resurrection of the Dead,
the world will hear us say

The phone is plugged in, please call,
I will answer it.

Catullus: Odi et amo

I hate *and* love. Ignorant fish, who even
wants the fly while writhing.

Confessional

Is she dead?

Yes, she is dead.

Did you forgive her?

No, I didn't forgive her.

Did she forgive you?

No, she didn't forgive me.

What did you have to forgive?

She was never mean, or willfully
cruel, or unloving.

When I was eleven, she converted to Christ—

she began to simplify her life, denied
herself, and said that she and I must struggle

"to divest ourselves
of the love of CREATED BEINGS,"—

and to help me to do that,

one day

        she hanged my cat.

I came home from school, and in the doorway
of my room,

my cat was hanging strangled.

She was in the bathroom; I could hear
the water running.

—I shouted at her;

                she wouldn't
come out.

        She was in there
for hours, with the water running . . .

Finally, late that night,
she unlocked the door.

                    She wouldn't look at me.

She said that we must learn to rest
in the LORD,—

and not in His CREATION . . .

        Did you forgive her?

Soon, she had a breakdown;
when she got out of the hospital,

she was SORRY . . .

For years she dreamed the cat
had dug
its claws into her thumbs:—

in the dream, she knew, somehow,
that it was dying; she tried

to help it,—

       TO PUT IT OUT OF ITS MISERY,—

so she had her hands around its
neck, strangling it . . .

           Bewildered,

it looked at her,

       KNOWING SHE LOVED IT—;

and she *DID* love it, which was
what was
       so awful . . .

All it could do was
hold on,—
      . . . AS
SHE HELD ON.

     Did you forgive her?

I was the center of her life,—
and therefore,
of her fears and obsessions. They changed;

one was money.

. . . DO I HAVE TO GO INTO IT?

Did you forgive her?

Standing next to her coffin, looking down
at her body, I suddenly
knew I hadn't—;

over and over
I said to her,

I didn't forgive you!
I didn't forgive you!

I *did* love her . . . Otherwise,

would I feel so guilty?

What did she have to forgive?

She was SORRY. She *tried*
to change . . .

She loved me. She was generous.

I pretended
that I had forgiven her—;

and she pretended
to believe it,—

she needed desperately to believe it . . .

SHE KNEW I COULD BARELY STAND TO BE AROUND HER.

Did you forgive her?

I *tried*—;
　　　　for years I almost
convinced myself I did . . .

But no, I didn't.

—Now, after I have said it all, so I can
rest,

　　　will you give me ABSOLUTION,—

. . . and grant this
　　　　　　　"created being"

FORGIVENESS? . . .

　　　Did she forgive you?

I think she tried—;
　　　　　　　but no,—
she *couldn't* forgive me . . .

WHY COULDN'T SHE FORGIVE ME?

　　　Don't you understand even now?

No! Not—not really . . .

　　　Forgiveness doesn't exist.

II

She asked,—

and I could not, WOULD NOT give . . .

—That is the first of two sentences
I can't get out of my head.

They somehow contain what happened.

The second is:—

THERE WAS NO PLACE IN NATURE WE COULD MEET.

Can you explain them?

Augustine too

had trouble with his mother,—

. . . LISTEN.

Confessor
incapable of granting *"rest"* or *"absolution,"*—

LISTEN . . .

Why are you angry?

Augustine too

had trouble with his mother,—

but the story of Augustine and Monica
is the *opposite* of what happened

between me and my mother . . .

We couldn't meet in Nature,—

. . . AND ALL WE HAD WAS NATURE.

How do you explain it?

The scene at the window at Ostia
in Book Nine of the *Confessions*

seems designed to make non-believers

sick with envy . . .

—You are listening to a soul
                         that has *always* been

SICK WITH ENVY . . .

How do you explain it?

As a child I was (now, I
clearly can see it)

PREDATORY,—

pleased to have supplanted my father
in my mother's affections,

and then pleased to have supplanted my stepfather . . .

—I assure you, though I was a *"little boy,"*
I could be far more charming, sympathetic,
full of sensibility, *"various,"* far more
an understanding and feeling
ear for my mother's emotions, needs, SOUL

than any man, any man she met,—

I know I *wanted* to be: WANTED
to be the center, the focus of her life . . .

I was her ally against my father;
and then, after the first two or three

years, her ally against my stepfather . . .

—Not long before she died,
she told me something
                    I had never heard,—

when I was nine or ten, early
in her second marriage,

she became pregnant; she said she
wanted to have the child . . .

She said that one day, when my stepfather
was playing golf, she was out walking the course

with him, and suddenly

a man fell from one of the huge trees
lining the fairways . . .

A group of men had been cutting limbs;
she saw one of them fall,
                    and for a long time

lie there screaming.

Later that day, she had a miscarriage . . .

—After saying all this, she
looked at me insistently and said,

"*I wanted to have the child.*"

But as she was telling me the story,
I kept thinking

THANK GOD THE MAN FELL,
THANK GOD SHE SAW HIM FALL AND HAD A MISCARRIAGE

AND THE CHILD DIED . . .

—I felt sick. I knew I was *GLAD*
the man fell, *GLAD* she saw him fall

and the child died . . .

—When I was nine or ten, if she
had had a child—; if

she and a child and my stepfather
had made a FAMILY

from which I *had* to be closed off,
the remnant of a rejected, erased past,—

(I never had anything in common with,
or even RESPECTED, my stepfather,—)

I would have gone crazy . . .

—How could she have *BETRAYED ME*
in that way? . . .

How do you explain it?

I felt sick. I felt ill at how
PREDATORY I was,—

(my feelings *STILL* were,—)

at the envy and violence I could
will NOT to feel,

but *COULDN'T* not feel . . .

—Augustine has the temerity, after
his mother dies,

to admit he is GLAD
she no longer wanted to be buried

next to her husband . . .

He thanks God
for ridding her of this "vain desire."

Why are you angry?

In the words of Ecclesiastes:—

"Her loves, her hates, her jealousies,—

these all

have perished, nor will she EVER AGAIN

TAKE PART
in whatever is done under the sun . . ."

My mother,—

. . . *JUST DIED*.

The emotions, the *"issues"* in her life
didn't come out somewhere, reached no culmination,
climax, catharsis, —

she *JUST DIED*.

She wanted them to—;
how can I talk about

the way in which, when I was young,

we seemed to be engaged in an ENTERPRISE
together, —

the enterprise of "figuring out the world,"
figuring out her life, my life, —

THE MAKING OF HER SOUL,

which somehow, in our "enterprise"
together, was the making of my soul, —

. . . it's a kind of *CRAZINESS*, which some mothers
drink along with their children
in their *MOTHER'S-MILK* . . .

Why are you angry?

THERE WAS NO PLACE IN NATURE WE COULD MEET . . .

—I've never let anyone else
in so deeply . . .

But when the predatory complicit co-conspirator
CHILD

was about twenty, he of course wanted his *"freedom,"*—

and then he found

that what had made his life
possible, what he found so deeply INSIDE HIM,

had its hands around his neck,

                        strangling him,—   .

and that therefore, if he were
to survive,

he must in turn strangle, murder,
kill it inside him . . .

TO SURVIVE, I HAD TO KILL HER INSIDE ME.

           Why are you angry?

Now that she is dead (that her BODY
is DEAD),

I'm capable of an *"empathy,"*

an *"acceptance"* of the INEVITABLE
(in her, and in myself)

that I denied her, living . . .

I DENIED HER, LIVING.

She asked,—

               and I could not, WOULD NOT give . . .

I *did* "will" to forgive her, but

FORGIVENESS lay beyond the will,—

. . . and I willed NOT to forgive her,
for "forgiveness" seems to say:—

Everything is forgotten, obliterated,—
                              the past
is as nothing, erased . . .

Her plea, her need for forgiveness
seemed the attempt to obliterate

the ACTIONS, ANGERS, DECISIONS

that *made me* what I am . . .

To obliterate the CRISES, FURIES, REFUSALS
that are how I
            came to *UNDERSTAND* her—; me—;

my life . . .

Truly to feel "forgiveness,"
to forgive her *IN MY HEART*,

                              meant erasing *ME* . . .

—She seemed to ask it to render me paralyzed,
and defenseless . . .

Now that I no longer must face her,
I give her in my mind

the *"empathy"* and *"acceptance"*

I denied her, living.

Why are you angry?

. . . But if, somehow, WHAT WE WERE
didn't have to be understood

by MEMORY,

      and THIS EARTH,—

. . . Augustine and Monica,

               as they lean
alone together standing at a window

overlooking a garden at the center of the house
(in Book Nine of the *Confessions*),

near the time of her death (which time,
Augustine says, GOD knew,

though they did not),—

resting here at Ostia from a long journey
by land,

and preparing for a long sea-journey
back to the Africa which is their home,—

. . . as they stand here sweetly talking together,
and ask

      "what the eternal life of the saints could be"

(panting to be sprinkled from the waters of God's fountain
to help them meditate
            upon so great a matter),—

. . . as they stand alone together
at this window,

        they can FORGET THE PAST

AND LOOK FORWARD

        TO WHAT LIES BEFORE THEM . . .

—They had much to forget;

in the *Confessions,* Monica's ferocity
is frightening:—

        before Augustine became a Christian,
she saw him as dead—;

she refused to live with him or even
eat at the same table in his house,
shunning and detesting his blasphemies,—

until she had a dream in which she
learned that he would finally convert to Christ . . .

—When he planned to leave Africa for Italy,
she was determined he would take her
with him, or remain at home;

she followed him to the seacoast,
clinging to him, he says, with *"dreadful grief"*;

one night he escaped,
        and sailed,—

not long after, she followed . . .

—Finally, of course, he became a Christian;
until then, she
ceaselessly wept and mourned and prayed . . .

Do you know why you are saying all this?

As Augustine and Monica stood leaning at that
window in Ostia, contemplating

what the saints' possession of God is like,

they moved past and reviewed
(Augustine tells us)

                each level of created things,—

each level of CREATION, from this earth
to the sun and moon and stars

shining down on this earth . . .

—Talking, musing, wondering
at Creation, but knowing that our life and light

here cannot compare

to the sweetness of the saints' LIGHT and LIFE,—

(here, where he had forced her to *SEEK*
what out of her body she had herself

brought forth,—)

. . . now, self-gathered at last in the purity of their own
being, they ascend higher

still, and together SCALE THE STARS . . .

—And so, Augustine tells us, they came to their own Souls,—

and then went
past them, to that region of richness

unending, where God feeds ISRAEL forever
with the food of Truth . . .

There LIFE is the WISDOM
by which all things are made, which

itself is *not* made . . .

—While they were thus talking of, straining to comprehend,
panting for this WISDOM, with all the effort

of their heart, for one heartbeat,

they together attained to *touch* it—;

. . . then sighing, and leaving the first-fruits
of their Spirit bound there,

they returned to the sound of their own voice,—
to WORDS,

which have a beginning and an end . . .

"How unlike," Augustine says, "God's WORD,—
changeless, self-gathered, unmade, yet forever

making all things new . . ."

　　　　How do you explain it?

Then they said:—
　　　　　　"If any man could shut his ears

to the tumult of the flesh—;

　　　　　　　　　if suddenly the cacophony
of earth and sea and air

were SILENT, and the voice of the self
died to the self, and so the self

found its way beyond the self,—

beyond the SELF it has made,—

                    SILENT
our expiations and confessions,
the voice that says: *NO REMISSION OF SINS
WITHOUT THE SHEDDING OF BLOOD*,

the WORD that was only given us drenched in blood,—

. . . if to any man

                    his Self, CREATION ITSELF

(Substance and Accidents and their Relations)

suddenly were SILENT,—

                    and in that silence,

he then heard CREATION
                    say with one voice:—

We are not our own source,—
                    even those of us

who made ourselves, creatures
of the Will, the Mirror, and the Dream,

know we are not our own source,—

. . . if he heard this voice,
                    and then

all Creation were, even for a second, SILENT,—

(this Creation in which creatures
of consciousness,

                        whose LAW is that they come to be
through CHANGE, through
birth, fruition, and death,

know that as they move toward fullness
of being, they move toward ceasing to be,—)

. . . if in this SILENCE,

He whom we *crave* to hear

                        SPOKE AT LAST—;

spoke not through the VEIL
of earth and sea and air,

thunder, 'SIGNS AND WONDERS,' the voice
of an angel, the enigma of similitude and of

parable, all

the ALIEN that BESETS us here,—

. . . spoke not by them, but by HIMSELF,

calling us to return into that secret place from
which He

                        comes forth at last to us,—

. . . just as we two
together reached forth and for one

heartbeat attained to *TOUCH*

the *WISDOM* that is our *SOURCE* and *GROUND*,—

. . . if this could continue, and LIFE
were that one moment of
                    wisdom and understanding

for which we then sighed,—

would not *this* be: *ENTER THOU INTO THE JOY OF THY LORD?* . . .

And when shall it be? At
the Resurrection of the Dead, when all
shall rise, but not all shall be changed?

And shall *we* then be changed? . . ."

In words like these, but not
exactly these, (Augustine then says,)

they talked together that day—

(just as the words I have given you are
not, of course, exactly Augustine's).

Monica then said,
                    "Son, I no longer hope

for anything from this world.

I wanted to stay alive long enough
to see you a Catholic Christian.

God has granted me this, in
superabundance.

. . . What am I still doing here?"

In five days, she fell into a fever;
nine days later she was dead.

Why are you angry?

My mother, at the end of her life, was *frightened.*

She was afraid to die
not because she feared an afterlife,

but because she didn't know what her life had been.

Her two marriages were failures,—

she stayed married to my stepfather, but
in despair, without trust in or respect for him, or

visible affection . . .

She had had no profession,—

she had painted a few paintings, and
written a handful of poems, but without the illusion

either were any good, or STOOD FOR HER . . .

She had *MADE* nothing.

I was what she had made.—

She saw that her concern and worry and care
in the end called up in me

protestations of affection
that veiled

        unappeasable anger, and remorse.

UNDOING THIS was beyond me . . .

She felt she was here for some REASON,—
. . . but never found it.

> *Man needs a metaphysics;*
> *he cannot have one.*

The Sacrifice

When Judas writes the history of SOLITUDE,—
. . . let him celebrate

Miss Mary Kenwood; who, without
help, placed her head in a plastic bag,

then locked herself
in a refrigerator.

                    .

—Six months earlier, after thirty years
teaching piano, she had watched

her mother slowly die of throat cancer.
Watched her *want* to die . . .

What once had given Mary life
in the end didn't want it.

Awake, her mother screamed for help to die.
—She felt

GUILTY . . . She knew that *all* men in these situations felt
innocent—; helpless—; yet guilty.

                    .

Christ knew the Secret. Betrayal
is necessary; as is woe for the betrayer.

The solution, Mary realized at last,
must be brought out of my own body.

Wiping away our sins, Christ stained us with his blood—;
to offer yourself, yet need *betrayal,* by *Judas,* before SHOULDERING

THE GUILT OF THE WORLD—;
. . . *Give me the courage not to need Judas.*

         •

When Judas writes the history of solitude,
let him record

that to the friend who opened
the refrigerator, it seemed

death fought; before giving in.

Genesis 1-2:4

In the beginning, God made HEAVEN and EARTH.

The earth without form was waste.

DARKNESS was the face of the deep.
His spirit was the wind brooding over the waters.

·

In darkness he said,
    LET THERE BE LIGHT.

There was light.

In light he said, IT IS GOOD.

God, dividing darkness from light,
named light DAY and darkness NIGHT.

Night and day were the first day.

·

God said,
    LET THE FIRMAMENT

ARC THE EARTH.

The waters opened.

The ARC above the earth
divided the waters above from the waters below.

God named the arc, HEAVEN.

Night and day were the second day.

          •

God said,
          LET THE WATERS BELOW THE FIRMAMENT

RECEDE, REVEALING THE GROUND.

The waters opened, and receded.
What lay beneath the waters was the GROUND.

God named the dry ground, EARTH.
He named the waters surrounding the earth, OCEAN.

God looked.
          He said, IT IS GOOD.

God said,
          LET THE BARE EARTH

BREAK OPEN, HEAVY WITH SEED.

The earth broke open.
                    Numberless PLANTS filled

with seed spread over the ground, and TREES
boughed with fruit heavy with seed.

God looked.
          He said, IT IS GOOD.

Night and day were the third day.

God said,
> LET GREAT LIGHTS IN THE FIRMAMENT

ORDER AND ILLUMINATE THE EARTH.

God placed great lights shining in the firmament,

the GREATER LIGHT to dominate the day,
the LESSER LIGHT to dominate the night,

and STARS.

God looked. He said,
> LET THEM BE FOR SIGNS.

Dividing darkness from light, the shining
made SEASONS, DAYS, YEARS.

God said, IT IS GOOD.

Night and day were the fourth day.

•

God said,
> LET THE MOVING WATERS LIVE

WITH TEEMING, LIVING CREATURES.

God said,
> LET THE EMPTY FIRMAMENT LIVE

WITH TEEMING, LIVING CREATURES.

God made the creatures of the deep,
BEASTS and MONSTERS, all those

swarming within it. God made the winged creatures
moving across the face of the firmament.

God looked.
   He said, IT IS GOOD.

God blessed them, saying,
       INCREASE. MULTIPLY.
FILL THE WATERS.
      ARCING THE EARTH,

FILL THE FIRMAMENT.

They increased and multiplied.

Night and day were the fifth day.

     •

God said,
   LET THE EARTH BRING FORTH

LIVING CREATURES BOUND TO THE EARTH.

God made the beasts of the earth,
cattle, each according to its kind.

He made the creatures that crawl on the earth,
reptiles, each according to its kind.

God looked.
   He said, IT IS GOOD.

God said,
   LET US MAKE MAN

LIKE US, IN OUR IMAGE AND LIKENESS.

God said,
LET THEM DOMINATE THE EARTH,

AND THE CREATURES OF THE EARTH.

God made MAN in his own image,
in the image of God

he made him,
MAN and WOMAN
he made them.

Of one likeness
MALE FE MALE
two he made.

God blessed them, saying,
INCREASE. MULTIPLY.

DOMINATE THE EARTH,

AND THE CREATURES OF THE EARTH.

God looked. He said,
YOUR MEAT SHALL BE

PLANTS, SEEDS, FRUIT.

God said to the man and woman
and all the creatures on the earth,

YOUR MEAT SHALL BE THE EARTH,

NOT THE CREATURES OF THE EARTH.

God looked.
He said, IT IS VERY GOOD.

Night and day were the sixth day.

·

God rested. On the seventh day

God rested. He looked at HEAVEN and EARTH,
and ceased.

Heaven and earth with all their panoply
were made.

God blessed the seventh day, God made
the seventh day a holy day,

because on the seventh day God rested, God ceased.

·

This was the creation of the world.

The Book of the Body

(1977)

The Arc

When I wake up,
                 I try to convince myself that my arm
isn't there—
           to retain my sanity.

Then I try to convince myself it is.

     •   •   •

INSTRUCTIONS

1. Always bandage *firmly.* The pressure should be constant over the entire stump with greatest pressure near the tip to attempt to make the stump cone-shaped.

2. If stump starts to *throb,* remove the bandage at once. Leave bandage off for one hour and rebandage the stump as before, *firmly.* Inspect the skin of your stump daily for any blisters, spots or sores and report them.

3. Wash bandage with mild soap in luke warm water. DO NOT WRING! Squeeze the waters out gently and place the bandage over the shower rod to dry thoroughly. DO NOT STRETCH OR IRON!!

4. Change the stump sock daily. Wash the sock daily with mild soap in luke warm water. DO NOT WRING! Squeeze the water out gently—place the sock on a flat surface to dry.

     •   •   •

I used to vaguely perceive the necessity
of coming to terms with the stump-filled, material world,—

things; bodies;
                    CRAP—

a world of accident, and chance—;

but after
the accident, I had to understand it

not as an accident—;

                    the way my mother,
years before locked in McLean's,

believed the painting of a snow-scene above her bed
had been placed there by the doctor to make her feel cold.

How could we *convince* her it had no point? . . .

It had no point,—
                    it was there
without relation to my mother; by chance; by
CHANCE the car swerved when a yellow car

came at us—; and the next
minute, when I looked down

all I saw was a space below the elbow
                    instead of my arm . . .

The police still can't figure out exactly what happened.

I tell myself:
"Insanity is the insistence on meaning."

                    •   •   •

He asked me if I wanted to get undressed, but I'm
embarrassed to take my shirt off,

so I told him to go ahead and take all his clothes off.

His body looked small and white lying on top of the dark bedspread.

I said I wanted to watch him wash
his prick.
        He got up and walked
to the washbasin against the wall,

then I went up, and started to wash
it with mild soap in luke warm water.
I squeezed it.
        He laughed,

and after drying off, went back to the bed.

I asked if he had a job.
        "Drove a truck for a while,
but about a week ago—I got laid off."

He looked uneasy, almost scared.
        "When I was in Vietnam,
my wife met someone else, and divorced me.
I have a little daughter three years old."

He got his wallet and showed me the little girl's picture.

"I don't blame my wife—I was gone
a long time, and like everybody
else in Vietnam I did a lot of fucking around."

He looked frightened and embarrassed, seeming to want
me to reassure him . . .
        I asked him to tell me about Vietnam.

"Anything you touched might explode. I know guys
just kicked a rock, and got killed . . .

Once a buddy of mine
was passing a hut, when a gook motioned to him to come inside.
Inside a woman was lying on her back, with
a pile of cigarettes next to her. He threw
some cigarettes on the pile, got on top of her,
and shoved in his prick.

He screamed.
She had a razor blade inside.

The whole end of his thing was sliced in two . . .

They fixed it up;

but what can he tell his wife?"

When he asked me what kind of sex I wanted,
I suddenly

forgot why

a body can make me feel horny—;

I wanted to leave.

But afraid
leaving might insult him, I asked him to masturbate.

"Sure."

He closed his eyes. For several minutes
his arm and hand with great energy
worked, as his contorted face tried to concentrate.

I stared at him, wishing
I could know
the image in his mind when at last he came.

•   •   •

The person I can't forget on my mother's ward
I don't know the name of.
                              She still stands there
in my mind,—

                  though it is summer, and hot,
she is wearing a heavy terry-cloth robe,
sweating, with a thin metal chain around her neck:

that's all—
            she is assuring me
she wears nothing under the robe,

that to wear anything
would *limit* her, that the doctors tell her
to have an "identity"
                      she must wear something—

"But I don't want an identity!

This way I'm *free* . . . Everybody else
has a medal on their chain, with a picture

or name on it, but I don't—
this way
I'm not bound down . . ."

With two hands
she begins to work the chain
around and around her neck, she soon gets
franticly excited,
                    and finally the attendant leads her away . . .

I only saw her once; that's
her identity in my mind,—

and even in my mind,

sweating
she wears a body.

     •   •   •

In Michelangelo's drawing *The Dream,* a man,

his arms lightly touching the globe,
all the masks at last lying dead beneath him,

is wakened by an angel
       hovering above him,

the angel's trumpet directed by the angel's arms,
the two figures connected by the trumpet,

wakened to the World ranged round him,
which is his dream, as well as Sin:

Sex. Identity. History. Family.
Affection. Obsession. Chance.

      —the seven
Deadly Sins, spirit
implicating itself in matter, only able to know itself
by what it has done in Time,—

are all ranged round him, the angel
waking him to himself . . . his arms lightly touching the globe.

     •   •   •

In Paris, on the footbridge between the Ile St. Louis
and the Ile de la Cité,

about six months after the accident,
I had an illumination:

the *solution* was to forget
that I had ever had an arm.
                          The lost arm had never existed.

Since the accident,
I had gotten more and more obsessed: the image
of what I had been,
                    the anticipations,
demands and predilections of a two-armed man
haunted me—

I was no longer whole; proportioned; inviolate . . .

In a store, I found a "memorial album":
birth date, death date, place
of rest, visitors to the coffin—
                          I could clearly see
an obituary:
            On a certain date, in a certain place,
            he lost his arm.

Twice I dreamed the cone of my stump
was a gravestone:
                 I *saw* it:
                          the whole of my life
was a kind of arc
stretching between two etched, ineradicable dates . . .

I had to escape that arc—

even notions like *career* and *marriage* (all those things
which because they
have a beginning, must end—)
                          seemed to suffocate . . .

I went to Paris. My family's sympathy,
the vivid scenes of my former life

whispered that my body was bound by two iron dates . . .

One day, leaving my hotel on the Ile St. Louis,
I saw a black dog and a young boy madly running.

Nothing unusual—
                    except the dog only had one
front leg. He seemed without consciousness
of what he lacked;
                    free of memory as a vegetable.

Looking at each other, they happily jogged along,
started to cross the bridge, and I followed—

then, as I crossed it, suddenly
I felt that I too must erase my past,
that I could, *must* pretend (almost
as an experiment) I had never had more
than one arm, that the image
faced in the mirror
was the only, the inevitable image . . .

—For a time, it worked;
                    I *was* happy;

without a past, I seemed not to exist
in time at all,—

I only remember a sense of release, ease,
proportion—
                    I am now one, not less than one . . .

Then, after about two weeks, imperceptibly
everything I saw became

cardboard . . .

Even the things I touched—
                              I couldn't allow myself to remember
the vivid associations
which gave dimension to what I
                              touched, saw, smelt,—

the resonance of every image
I had to try to cut from my brain, it had been felt
by someone with two hands and two arms . . .

I had to try to cut from my brain
                              my phantom hand
which still gets cramps, which my brain still
recognizes as real—

                    and now, I think of Paris,

how Paris is still the city of Louis XVI and
Robespierre, how blood, amputation, and rubble

give her dimension, resonance, and grace.

Happy Birthday

Thirty-three, goodbye—
the awe I feel

is not that you won't come again, or why—

or even that after
a time, we think of those who are dead

with a sweetness that cannot be explained—

but that I've read the trading-cards:
RALPH TEMPLE CYCLIST CHAMPION TRICK RIDER

WILLIE HARRADON CYCLIST
THE YOUTHFUL PHENOMENON

F. F. IVES CYCLIST
100 MILES 6 H. 25 MIN. 30 SEC.

—as the fragile metal of their
wheels stopped turning, as they

took on wives, children, accomplishments, all those
predilections which also insisted on ending,

they could not tell themselves from what they had done.

Terrible to dress in the clothes
of a period that must end.

They didn't plan it that way—
they didn't plan it that way.

Elegy

I. Belafont

"He seemed to have gotten better—

> Tuesday, for the first time
> in a week, he went out
> into the front yard, and
> pottied by lifting his leg—

which he hadn't had

the strength to do. So we left him

just for an hour—

the vet says
somebody must have
got to him again, in
that hour—

> one in the morning, he started to
> cough, throw up, and Floyd
> stayed with him
> all night—

> at six, he called the vet, and at ten
> he died.

He had a *good* life—

you feel so guilty, even though you
did all you could—

                  I talked
                  to my doctor, and

he says you
always feel that way, though you
did all you
humanly could—all you
humanly could—"

(*pause*) "He had a *good* life—"

                    My mother's dog is dead;
                    as truly as I am, he was her son;
                    we used to laugh at the comparison.

"When your father was drunk one night,
he started to hit me; you were only five, but
stood up to him, and said:
                  'If you ever
try to hit mommy again, I'll kill you.'

I knew then I *had* to leave.

When we came to the city,
you were a real toughie—
                  I'll never forget the first
day of kindergarten, you were sent home because
you called the lady teacher a 'sonofabitch'!

—You'd only been around cowboys;
but later, you only wanted to be with me.

I had to *push* you away—

we were always
more like each other than anyone else."

We used to laugh at the comparison.

"I insisted they bury him here, in the garden: Floyd
made a box: we wrapped him

in one of our best
white sheets."—Was it his fault

they loved him
more than each other? Or their fault

their love
forbade him in his nine years

from even licking his genitals?
She got him

the year before I went away to school,
"to take your place,"

she kidded. She used to laugh
at poodles on the street—clipped, manicured,

clung to.
But what was she to do—

change, or have another child?

Belafont, I saw you in a dream tonight,
reaching toward me to kiss me

but carefully avoiding the mouth, as
taught,

yet constantly, defiantly skirting it—
then plunging into a pile of old, empty shoeboxes

to come up with the strap
I wear on my weak

left wrist
exercising each night, remaking

the embarrassing
soft overfed unloved body

I try to blame on the past—;
tilting your head, the strap

hanging from one side of the mouth,
you look at me with your

daring, lawless
stare—

and begin to chew.

II. Pruning

"I'd rather die than let them
take off a breast. I'd rather die
than go through cobalt again."

She means it,—
                 but I can't help but remember
her at least fifteen years earlier,

standing in the doorway, shrieking at me
when I wanted to be a priest:
                          "It's just as well!

You had mumps—; they went down—; you'll never,
gelding, have kids!"
                          twisting her last knife

to save me from the Church, the Church
which called her remarriage adultery . . .

—She is saying: "If the cancer
pops out somewhere else, I won't let them operate.
I'd rather die.
                 They just
butcher you . . . Besides, it never works."

III. Lover

"I'll be right over."
"Give me a few minutes: I'm still

in my pajamas."
"Don't get out of your pajamas."

"Don't get out of my pajamas?"
"—Don't get out of your pajamas!"

And so we learned how to make two lovers
of friends; now,

caught "between a rock and a hard place—" (after
the hospital, after

"gestation" was "interrupted") we still
when we call even say we love each other . . .

Too bad two people don't have to "love each other"
more, to make a child.

IV. Light

I am asleep, dreaming a terrible dream, so I awake,
and want to call my father to ask if, just
for a short time, the dog can come to stay with me.

But the light next to my bed won't light:
I press and press the switch. Touching the phone,
I can't see to dial the numbers. Can I learn how to keep

the dog in my apartment? In the dark, trying
a second light, I remember
I always knew these machines would fail me.

                                    Then I awake,

remember my father and the dog are dead,
the lights in that room do not go on.

V. Lineage

"I went to a mausoleum today, and found
what I want. Eye-level.
Don't forget:
I want to be buried in a mausoleum at eye-level."

She feels she never quite recovered
from her mother's, my grandmother's, death.

Her mother died by falling from a
third floor hospital window.

"—I'm *sure* she didn't want to kill herself;

after the stroke, sometimes she got confused, and
maybe she thought
                    she saw grandpa at the window . . .

She wanted to be at home. After the stroke,
we *had* to put her in a nursing home,—

she hated it, but you couldn't
get help to stay with her, and she needed
someone twenty-four hours a day,—

she begged me to take her out;
                              the cruel,
unreasonable things she said to me! Her doctor

told me I was doing the right thing, but
what she said
                almost drove me crazy . . .

it's astonishing how clearly I can still hear her voice.

I still dream I can see her falling
three stories, her arms stretching out . . .

For forty years, she counted
on grandpa,—
                after he died, she still
talked to him.

I know I made a lot of
mistakes with you, but I couldn't count on anyone—

I had to be both father *and* mother . . ."

As the subject once again changes from my grandmother

to my father, or the dog—
to my stepfather, or me—
                her obsessive, baffled voice

says that when she allowed herself to love

she let something into her head which will
never be got out—;
                which could only betray her
or *be* betrayed, but never appeased—;
whose voice

                death and memory have made
into a razor-blade without a handle . . .

"Don't forget:
I want to be buried in a mausoleum at eye-level."

Envoi

"If it resists me, I know it's real—"
a friend said. I thought of you . . . When I said,
"I feel too much. I can't stand what I feel"

I meant, as always, facing you.—You're real;
and smile at me no *less* woundedly, dead.
If it resists me, I know it's real.

Now no act of Mind,—or Will,—can reveal
the secret to *un-say* all we once said . . .
I feel too much. I can't stand what I feel.

The only way we stumbled to the Real
was through failure; outrage; betrayals; dread.
If it resists me, I know it's real.

Is the only salvation through what's real?
But each book . . . reads me—; who remains unread.
I feel too much. I can't stand what I feel.

Mother, I didn't forgive you. Conceal
unreal forgiving. Show me your face in fury—; not dead.
If it resists me, I know it's real.
I feel too much. I can't stand what I feel.

The Book of the Body

Wanting to cease to feel—;

since 1967,
so much blood under the bridge,—

the deaths of both my parents,
(now that they have no
body, only when I have no body

can we meet—)

my romance with Orgasm,

exhilaration like Insight, but without
content?—

the NO which is YES, the YES which is NO—

Daphnis,
astonished at the unaccustomed threshold of heaven,

in his whiteness
sees beneath his feet the clouds and stars . . .

—So many
infatuations guaranteed to fail before they started,

terror at my own homosexuality,

terror which somehow
evaporated slowly with "Gay Liberation"

and finding that I had fathered a child—;

. . . All those who loved me
whom I did not want;

all those whom I loved
who did not want me;

all those whose love I reciprocated

but in a way somehow
                    unlike what they wanted . . .

—Blindness. Blankness.
A friend said, "I've hurt so many . . ." And

for what?
                    to what *end?—*

An adult's forgiveness of his parents
born out of increasing age and empathy

which really forgives nothing,—
but is loathing, rage, revenge,

yet forgiveness as well—;

Sex the type of all action,

reconciliation with the body that is
annihilation of the body,

My romance with pornography,

watching it happen, watching

two bodies trying to make it happen,
however masterful or gorgeous, helpless

climbing the un-mappable mountain
of FEELING, the will

in sweat, hurt, exhaustion, accepting
limits of will,

the NO which is YES, the YES which is NO.

1974.

Ellen West

I love sweets,—
                    heaven
would be dying on a bed of vanilla ice cream . . .

But my true self
is thin, all profile

and effortless gestures, the sort of blond
elegant girl whose
                    body is the image of her soul.

—My doctors tell me I must give up
this ideal;
            but I
WILL NOT . . . cannot.

Only to my husband I'm not simply a "case."

But he is a fool. He married
meat, and thought it was a wife.

                ·   ·   ·

Why am I a girl?

I ask my doctors, and they tell me they
don't know, that it is just "given."

But it has such
implications—;

                and sometimes,
I even feel like a girl.

              •   •   •

Now, at the beginning of Ellen's thirty-second year, her physical
condition has deteriorated still further. Her use of laxatives increases
beyond measure. Every evening she takes sixty to seventy tablets of
a laxative, with the result that she suffers tortured vomiting at night
and violent diarrhea by day, often accompanied by a weakness of the
heart. She has thinned down to a skeleton, and weighs only 92
pounds.

              •   •   •

About five years ago, I was in a restaurant,
eating alone
              with a book. I was
not married, and often did that . . .

—I'd turn down
dinner invitations, so I could eat alone;

I'd allow myself two pieces of bread, with
butter, at the beginning, and three scoops of
vanilla ice cream, at the end,—

                        sitting there alone
with a book, both in the book
and out of it, waited on, idly
watching people,—

                  when an attractive young man
and woman, both elegantly dressed,
sat next to me.
              She was beautiful—;

with sharp, clear features, a good
bone structure—;
                    if she took her make-up off
in front of you, rubbing cold cream
again and again across her skin, she still would be
beautiful—
          more beautiful.

And he,—
          I couldn't remember when I had seen a man
so attractive. I didn't know why. He was almost

a male version
          of her,—

I had the sudden, mad notion that I
wanted to be his lover . . .

—Were they married?
                    were *they* lovers?

They didn't wear wedding rings.

Their behavior was circumspect. They discussed
politics. They didn't touch . . .

—How could I discover?

                    Then, when the first course
arrived, I noticed the way

each held his fork out for the other

to taste what he had ordered . . .

                    They did this
again and again, with pleased looks, indulgent
smiles, for each course,

more than once for *each* dish—;
much too much for just friends . . .

—Their behavior somehow sickened me;

the way each *gladly*
put the *food* the other had offered *into his mouth*—;

I knew what they were. I knew they slept together.

An immense depression came over me . . .

—I knew I could never
with such ease allow another to put food into my mouth:

happily *myself* put food into another's mouth—;

I knew that to become a wife I would have to give up my ideal.

      •   •   •

Even as a child,
I saw that the "natural" process of aging

is for one's middle to thicken—
one's skin to blotch;

as happened to my mother.
And her mother.
             I loathed "Nature."

At twelve, pancakes
became the most terrible thought there is . . .

I shall *defeat* "Nature."

In the hospital, when they
weigh me, I wear weights secretly sewn into my belt.

·   ·   ·

January 16. The patient is allowed to eat in her room, but comes
readily with her husband to afternoon coffee. Previously she had
stoutly resisted this on the ground that she did not really eat but
devoured like a wild animal. This she demonstrated with utmost
realism. . . . Her physical examination showed nothing striking.
Salivary glands are markedly enlarged on both sides.

January 21. Has been reading *Faust* again. In her diary, writes
that art is the "mutual permeation" of the "world of the body" and
the "world of the spirit." Says that her own poems are "hospital
poems . . . weak—without skill or perseverance; only managing to
beat their wings softly."

February 8. Agitation, quickly subsided again. Has attached
herself to an elegant, very thin female patient. Homo-erotic compo-
nent strikingly evident.

February 15. Vexation, and torment. Says that her mind forces
her always to think of eating. Feels herself degraded by this. Has
entirely, for the first time in years, stopped writing poetry.

·   ·   ·

Callas is my favorite singer, but I've only
seen her once—;

I've never forgotten that night . . .

—It was in *Tosca*, she had long before
lost weight, her voice
had been, for years,
                    deteriorating, half itself . . .

When her career began, of course, she was fat,

enormous—; in the early photographs,
sometimes I almost don't recognize her . . .

The voice too then was enormous—

healthy; robust; subtle; but capable of
crude effects, even vulgar,

                              almost out of
high spirits, too much health . . .

But soon she felt that she must lose weight,—
that all she was trying to express

was obliterated by her body,
buried in flesh—;

                    abruptly, within
four months, she lost at least sixty pounds . . .

—The gossip in Milan was that Callas
had swallowed a tapeworm.

But of course she hadn't.

                    The *tapeworm*
was her *soul* . . .

—How her soul, uncompromising,
insatiable,

            must have loved eating the flesh from her bones,

revealing this extraordinarily
mercurial; fragile; masterly creature . . .

—But irresistibly, nothing
stopped there; the huge voice

also began to change: at first, it simply diminished
in volume, in size,

                    then the top notes became
shrill, unreliable—at last,
usually not there at all . . .

—No one knows *why*. Perhaps her mind,
ravenous, still insatiable, sensed

that to struggle with the *shreds* of a voice

must make her artistry subtler, more refined,
more capable of expressing humiliation,
rage, betrayal . . .

—Perhaps the opposite. Perhaps her spirit
loathed the unending struggle

to *embody* itself, to *manifest* itself, on a stage whose

mechanics, and suffocating customs,
seemed expressly designed to annihilate spirit . . .

—I know that in *Tosca,* in the second act,
when, humiliated, hounded by Scarpia,
she sang *Vissi d'arte*
                        —"I lived for art"—

and in torment, bewilderment, at the end she asks,
with a voice reaching
                        harrowingly for the notes,

"Art has *repaid* me LIKE THIS?"

                                    I felt I was watching
autobiography—
                an art; skill;
virtuosity

miles distant from the usual soprano's
athleticism,—
                the usual musician's dream
of virtuosity *without* content . . .

—I wonder what she feels, now,
listening to her recordings.

For they have already, within a few years,
begun to date . . .

Whatever they express
they express through the style of a decade
and a half—;
                    a style *she* helped create . . .

—She must know that now
she probably would *not* do a trill in
exactly that way,—
                    that the whole sound, atmosphere,
dramaturgy of her recordings

have just slightly become those of the past . . .

—Is it bitter? Does her soul
tell her

that she was an *idiot* ever to think
anything
                    material wholly could satisfy? . . .

—Perhaps it says: *The only way*
to escape
the History of Styles

is not to have a body.

                    •   •   •

When I open my eyes in the morning, my great
mystery
                    stands before me . . .

—I *know* that I am intelligent; therefore

the inability not to fear food
day-and-night; this unending hunger
ten minutes after I have eaten . . .
                              a childish
dread of eating; hunger which can have no cause,—

half my mind says that all this
is *demeaning* . . .

                 Bread
for days on end
drives all real thought from my brain . . .

—Then I think, No. The ideal of being thin

conceals the ideal
not to have a body—;
                    which is NOT trivial . . .

This wish seems now as much a "given" of my existence

as the intolerable
fact that I am dark-complexioned; big-boned;
and once weighed
one hundred and sixty-five pounds . . .

—But then I think, *No.* That's too simple,—

without a body, who can
know himself at all?
                    Only by
acting; choosing; rejecting; have I
made myself—
                    discovered who and what *Ellen* can be . . .

—But then again I think, NO. This *I* is anterior

to name; gender; action;
fashion;
       MATTER ITSELF,—

. . . trying to stop my hunger with FOOD
is like trying to appease thirst
               with ink.

       •   •   •

March 30. Result of the consultation: Both gentlemen agree completely with my prognosis and doubt any therapeutic usefulness of commitment even more emphatically than I. All three of us are agreed that it is not a case of obsessional neurosis and not one of manic-depressive psychosis, and that no definitely reliable therapy is possible. We therefore resolved to give in to the patient's demand for discharge.

       •   •   •

The train-ride yesterday
was far *worse* than I expected . . .

                   In our compartment
were ordinary people: a student;
a woman; her child;—

they had ordinary bodies, pleasant faces;
                  but I thought
I was surrounded by creatures

with the pathetic, desperate
desire to be *not* what they were:—

the student was short,
and carried his body as if forcing
it to be taller—;

the woman showed her gums when she smiled,
and often held her
hand up to hide them—;

the child
seemed to cry simply because it was
small; a dwarf, and helpless . . .

—I was hungry. I had insisted that my husband
not bring food . . .

After about thirty minutes, the woman
peeled an orange

to quiet the child. She put a section
into its mouth—;
                    immediately it spit it out.

The piece fell to the floor.

—She pushed it with her foot through the dirt
toward me
several inches.

My husband saw me staring
down at the piece . . .

—I didn't move; how I wanted
to reach out,
                    and as if invisible

shove it in my mouth—;

my body
became rigid. As I stared at him,
I could see him staring

at me,—
　　　then he looked at the student—; at the woman—; then
back to me . . .

I didn't move.

—At last, he bent down, and
casually
　　　threw it out the window.

He looked away.

—I got up to leave the compartment, then
saw his face,—

his eyes
were red;
　　　and I saw

—*I'm sure I saw*—

disappointment.

•　　　•　　　•

On the third day of being home she is as if transformed. At breakfast
she eats butter and sugar, at noon she eats so much that—for the first
time in thirteen years!—she is satisfied by her food and gets really
full. At afternoon coffee she eats chocolate creams and Easter eggs.
She takes a walk with her husband, reads poems, listens to record-
ings, is in a positively festive mood, and all heaviness seems to have
fallen away from her. She writes letters, the last one a letter to the
fellow patient here to whom she had become so attached. In the
evening she takes a lethal dose of poison, and on the following
morning she is dead. "She looked as she had never looked in life
—calm and happy and peaceful."

•　　　•　　　•

Dearest.—I remember how
at eighteen,
             on hikes with friends, when
they rested, sitting down to joke or talk,

I circled
around them, afraid to hike ahead alone,

yet afraid to rest
when I was not yet truly thin.

You and, yes, my husband,—
you and he

have by degrees drawn me within the circle;
forced me to sit down at last on the ground.

I am grateful.

But something in me *refuses* it.

—How eager I have been
to compromise, to kill this *refuser*,—

but each compromise, each attempt
to poison an ideal
which often seemed to *me* sterile and unreal,

heightens my hunger.

I am crippled. I disappoint you.

Will you greet with anger, or
happiness,

the news which might well reach you
before this letter?

                    Your *Ellen.*

Golden State

(1973)

PART ONE

Herbert White

"When I hit her on the head, it was good,

and then I did it to her a couple of times,—
but it was funny,—afterwards,
it was as if somebody else did it . . .

Everything flat, without sharpness, richness or line.

Still, I liked to drive past the woods where she lay,
tell the old lady and the kids I had to take a piss,
hop out and do it to her . . .

The whole buggy of them waiting for me
                              made me feel good;
but still, just like I knew all along,
                              she didn't move.

When the body got too discomposed,
I'd just jack off, letting it fall on her . . .

—It sounds crazy, but I tell you
sometimes it was *beautiful*—; I don't know how
to say it, but for a minute, *everything* was possible—;
and then,
then,—
        well, like I said, she didn't move: and I saw,
under me, a little girl was just lying there in the mud:

and I knew I couldn't have done that,—
somebody *else* had to have done that,—

standing above her there,

in those ordinary, shitty leaves . . .

—One time, I went to see Dad in a motel where he was
staying with a woman; but she was gone;
you could smell the wine in the air; and he started,
real embarrassing, to cry . . .

He was still a little drunk,
and asked me to forgive him for
all he hadn't done—; but, What the shit?
Who would have wanted to stay with Mom? with bastards
not even his own kids?

I got in the truck, and started to drive,
and saw a little girl—
who I picked up, hit on the head, and
screwed, and screwed, and screwed, and screwed, then

buried,

in the garden of the motel . . .

—You see, ever since I was a kid I wanted
to *feel* things make sense: I remember

looking out the window of my room back home,—
and being almost suffocated by the asphalt;
and grass; and trees; and glass;
just *there*, just *there*, doing nothing!
not saying anything! filling me up—
but also being a wall; dead, and stopping me;
—how I wanted to see beneath it, cut

beneath it, and make it
somehow, come alive . . .

The salt of the earth;
Mom once said, 'Man's spunk is the salt of the earth . . .'

—That night, at that Twenty-nine Palms Motel
I had passed a million times on the road, everything

fit together; was alright;
it seemed like
            everything *had* to be there, like I had spent years
trying, and at last finally finished drawing this
                      huge circle . . .

—But then, suddenly I knew
somebody *else* did it, some bastard
had hurt a little girl—; the motel
                 I could see again, it had been
itself all the time, a lousy
pile of bricks, plaster, that didn't seem to
have to be there,—but *was,* just by chance . . .

—Once, on the farm, when I was a kid,
I was screwing a goat; and the rope around his neck
when he tried to get away
pulled tight;—and just when I came,
he *died* . . .
           I came back the next day; jacked off over his body;
but it didn't do any good . . .

Mom once said:
'Man's spunk is the salt of the earth, and grows kids.'

I tried so hard to come; more *pain* than anything else;
but didn't do any good . . .

—About six months ago, I heard Dad remarried,
so I drove over to Connecticut to see him and see
if he was happy.
           She was twenty-five years younger than him:
she had lots of little kids, and I don't know why,
I felt shaky . . .

I stopped in front of the address; and
snuck up to the window to look in . . .
                              —There he was, a kid
six months old on his lap, laughing
and bouncing the kid, happy in his old age
to play the papa after years of sleeping around,—
it twisted me up . . .
   .   To think that what he wouldn't give me,
                       he *wanted* to give them . . .

          I could have killed the bastard . . .

—Naturally, I just got right back in the car,
and believe me, was determined, determined,
to head straight for home . . .

                              but the more I drove,
I kept thinking about getting a girl,
and the more I thought I shouldn't do it,
the more I had to—

                       I saw her coming out of the movies,
saw she was alone, and
kept circling the blocks as she walked along them,
saying, 'You're going to leave her alone.'
'You're going to leave her alone.'

                              —The woods were scary!
As the seasons changed, and you saw more and more
of the skull show through, the nights became clearer,
and the buds,—erect, like nipples . . .

—But then, one night,
nothing *worked* . . .
                  Nothing in the sky
would blur like I wanted it to;
and I couldn't, *couldn't,*

get it to seem to me
that somebody *else* did it . . .

I tried, and tried, but there was just me there,
and her, and the sharp trees
saying, 'That's you standing there.
                            You're . . .
                                            just you.'

                    I hope I fry.

—Hell came when I saw
                    MYSELF . . .
                                        and couldn't stand
what I see . . .''

Self-Portrait, 1969

He's *still* young—; thirty, but looks younger—
or does he? . . . In the eyes and cheeks, tonight,
turning in the mirror, he saw his mother,—
puffy; angry; bewildered . . . Many nights
now, when he stares there, he gets angry:—
something *unfulfilled* there, something dead
to what he once thought he surely could be—
Now, just the glamour of habits . . .

                                    Once, instead,
he thought insight would remake him, he'd reach
—what? The thrill, the exhilaration
unravelling disaster, that seemed to teach
necessary knowledge . . . became just jargon.

Sick of being decent, he craves another
crash. What *reaches* him except disaster?

PART TWO

California Plush

The only thing I miss about Los Angeles

is the Hollywood Freeway at midnight, windows down and
radio blaring
bearing right into the center of the city, the Capitol Tower
on the right, and beyond it, Hollywood Boulevard
blazing

—pimps, surplus stores, footprints of the stars

—descending through the city
                    fast as the law would allow

through the lights, then rising to the stack
out of the city
to the stack where lanes are stacked six deep

            and you on top; the air
            now clean; for a moment weightless

                    without memories, or
                    need for a past.

The need for the past

is so much at the center of my life
I write this poem to record my discovery of it,
my reconciliation.

                    It was in Bishop, the room was done
in California plush: we had gone into the coffee shop, were told
you could only get a steak in the bar:
                                        I hesitated,
not wanting to be an occasion of temptation for my father

but he wanted to, so we entered

a dark room, with amber water glasses, walnut
tables, captain's chairs,
plastic doilies, papier-mâché bas-relief wall ballerinas,
German memorial plates "bought on a trip to Europe,"
Puritan crosshatch green-yellow wallpaper,
frilly shades, cowhide
booths—

I thought of Cambridge:

                the lovely congruent elegance
                of Revolutionary architecture, even of

ersatz thirties Georgian

seemed alien, a threat, sign
of all I was not—

to bode order and lucidity

as an ideal, if not reality—

not this California plush, which

                    also

I was not.

And so I made myself an Easterner,
finding it, after all, more like me
than I had let myself hope.

And now, staring into the embittered face of
    my father,

again, for two weeks, as twice a year,
    I was back.

            The waitress asked us if we wanted a drink.
Grimly, I waited until he said no . . .

Before the tribunal of the world I submit the following
document:

            Nancy showed it to us,
in her apartment in the motel,
as she waited month by month
for the property settlement, her children grown
and working for their father,
at fifty-three now alone,
a drink in her hand:

            as my father said,
"They keep a drink in her hand":

                        Name Wallace Du Bois
                        Box No 128   *Chino, Calif.*
                        Date July 25   *,19* 54

Mr Howard Arturian
    I am writing a letter to you this afternoon while I'm in the
mood of writing. How is everything getting along with you these
fine days, as for me everything is just fine and I feel great except for
the heat I think its lot warmer then it is up there but I don't mind
it so much. I work at the dairy half day and I go to trade school the
other half day Body & Fender, now I am learning how to spray
paint cars I've already painted one and now I got another car to
paint. So now I think I've learned all I want after I have learned all

this. I know how to straighten metals and all that. I forgot to say
"Hello" to you. The reason why I am writing to you is about a job,
my Parole Officer told me that he got letter from and that you want
me to go to work for you. So I wanteded to know if its truth. When
I go to the Board in Feb. I'll tell them what I want to do and where
I would like to go, so if you want me to work for you I'd rather have
you sent me to your brother John in Tonapah and place to stay for
my family. The Old Lady says the same thing in her last letter that
she would be some place else then in Bishop, thats the way I feel
too. and another thing is my drinking problem. I made up my mind
to quit my drinking, after all what it did to me and what happen.

This is one thing I'll never forget as longs as I live I never want
to go through all this mess again. This sure did teach me lot of things
that I never knew before. So Howard you can let me know soon
as possible. I sure would appreciate it.

P. S   From Your Friend
I hope you can read my   Wally Du Bois
writing. I am a little nervous yet

—He and his wife had given a party, and
one of the guests was walking away
just as Wallace started backing up his car.
He hit him, so put the body in the back seat
and drove to a deserted road.
There he put it before the tires, and
ran back and forth over it several times.

When he got out of Chino, he did,
indeed, never do that again:
but one child was dead, his only son,
found with the rest of the family
immobile in their beds with typhoid,
next to the mother, the child having been
dead two days:

he continued to drink, and as if it were the Old West
shot up the town a couple of Saturday nights.

"So now I think I've learned all I want
after I have learned all this: this sure did teach me a lot of things
that I never knew before.
I am a little nervous yet."

It seems to me
an emblem of Bishop—

For watching the room, as the waitresses in their
back-combed, Parisian, peroxided, bouffant hairdos,
and plastic belts,
moved back and forth

I thought of Wallace, and
the room suddenly seemed to me
        not uninteresting at all:

        they were the same. Every plate and chair

        had its congruence with

        all the choices creating

        these people, created

        by them—by me,

for this is my father's chosen country, my origin.

Before, I had merely been anxious, bored; now,
I began to ask a thousand questions . . .

He was, of course, mistrustful, knowing I was bored,
knowing he had dragged me up here from Bakersfield

after five years

of almost managing to forget Bishop existed.

But he soon became loquacious, ordered a drink,
and settled down for
an afternoon of talk . . .

He liked Bishop: somehow, it was to his taste, this
hard-drinking, loud, visited-by-movie-stars town.
"Better to be a big fish in a little pond."

And he was: when they came to shoot a film,
he entertained them; Miss A——, who wore
nothing at all under her mink coat; Mr. M——,
good horseman, good shot.

"But when your mother
let me down" (for alcoholism and
infidelity, she divorced him)
"and Los Angeles wouldn't give us water any more,
I had to leave.

We were the first people to grow potatoes in this valley."

When he began to tell me
that he lost control of the business
because of the settlement he gave my mother,

because I had heard it
many times,

in revenge, I asked why people up here drank so much.

He hesitated. "Bored, I guess.
—Not much to do."

And why had Nancy's husband left her?

In bitterness, all he said was:
"People up here drink too damn much."

And that was how experience
had informed his life.

"So now I think I've learned all I want
after I have learned all this: this sure did teach me a lot of things
that I never knew before.
I am a little nervous yet."

Yet, as my mother said,
returning, as always, to the past,

"I wouldn't change any of it.
It taught me so much. Gladys
is such an innocent creature: you look into her face
and somehow it's empty, all she worries about
are sales and the baby.
Her husband's too good!"

It's quite pointless to call this rationalization:
my mother, for uncertain reasons, has had her
bout with insanity, but she's right:

the past in maiming us,
makes us,
fruition
          is also
destruction:

          I think of Proust, dying
in a cork-lined room, because he refuses to eat
because he thinks that he cannot write if he eats
because he wills to write, to finish his novel

—his novel which recaptures the past, and
with a kind of joy, because
in the debris
of the past, he has found the sources of the necessities

which have led him to this room, writing

—in this strange harmony, does he will
for it to have been different?

And I can't *not* think of the remorse of Oedipus,

who tries to escape, to expiate the past
by blinding himself, and
then, when he is dying, sees that he has become a Daimon

—does he, discovering, at last, this cruel
coherence created by
"the order of the universe"

—does he will
anything reversed?

I look at my father:
as he drinks his way into garrulous, shaky
defensiveness, the debris of the past
is just debris—; whatever I reason, it is a desolation
to watch . . .

must I watch?
He will not change; he does not *want* to change;

every defeated gesture implies
the past is useless, irretrievable . . .
—I want to change: I want to stop fear's subtle

guidance of my life—; but, how can I do that
if I am still
afraid of its source?

1966–67.

Book of Life

I once knew a man named Snake.

He killed
All our snakes.

        One day one bit him.

"Ha-ya feelin', Snake?"
I asked when he returned.

He said,
"My name is Walter."

            The brown house
            on the brown hill
            reminds me of my parents.

Its memory is of poverty,
not merely poverty of means,
but poverty of history, of awareness of
the ways men have found to live.

        My stepfather was from Texas.

"Niggers, you know they're different from us,
they go mad when they make love,
we white men have to watch out or women

won't have anything to do with us."

(*pause*) "Back in McKinney, there's a spot on the pavement
where they caught a nigger who'd raped a white woman,
right there they tied him down,
poured gasoline on him, and
lit him afire.
—You can still see the mark."

Illuminated by the lore of the past, justified
by the calluses on his hands,
—won walking round and round
a wheel digging a water
well fourteen hours a day—
he was happy with himself.

Before my mother married him, she was
free for several years, proposed to
by several men we may call,
in this context,

"educated"

(a lawyer; a doctor; unconfident men
sharing a certain unmistakable
humaneness)

and later, she often asked herself

why she married him.

She would laugh, and say, "I always liked the horse's asses!"

(*pause*) "My mother never told me about these things."

Its memory is of poverty,
not merely poverty of means,
but poverty of history, of awareness of
the ways men have found to live.

My father
"was the handsomest man in Kern County."

When they met, he was eight years older, and

driving a truck for a bootlegger.

He had had a dance studio in Hollywood,
gone broke, and

was back. "He introduced me to a fast, drinking crowd; my God,

we smoked—! And I wore lipstick: Olive and I promised each other

we would never do that."

So he went back into farming, as he had done as a child
when his father died, and
"was a genius."

"Your father, on our wedding night, told me
he had ninety-two thousand dollars in the bank. His first
potato crop. He didn't have a dime the year before."

But he
spent all the afternoons in the cool bars.
"He always was a sucker for a no-good
bum with a slick line and a good story.
How an intelligent man like that—"

Soon he
was an alcoholic, and unfaithful; unfaithful
many times; which fact was, as it were,

brought home to her, by
detectives. She would shake her head:

"How an intelligent man like that—"

(*bitterly*) "He never would have made us a real home,
the way decent men do."

In her own illness, when she began to
try to turn brass and tin into gold
by boiling them in a large pot full of
soap, cat's fur, and orange rinds,

she was following

the teachings of the Rosicrucians,

the secrets of the past, the mysteries of the

pyramids.

       Later, as she began
       to be well, she would ask,

"Why did it happen?

             It seems to
say something awful about
everything I've done.
            Does it make everything wrong?
I knew so little
all along!"

(*pause*) "Why did it happen to *me*— at

forty-eight?"

Its memory is of poverty,
not merely poverty of means,
but poverty of history, of awareness of
the ways men have found to live.

                                    For men are not
                                    children, who learn
                                    not to touch the burner; men,

unlike Walter,
cannot simply revert

to their true names.
                        The brown clapboard house,
in spite of its fine pioneer tradition,
because of the absence of the knowledge in its
lines of other architecture, because of the
poverty of its

brown, barren hill,

reminds me of my parents.

                                                    1966.

Golden State

I

To see my father
lying in pink velvet, a rosary
twined around his hands, rouged,
lipsticked, his skin marble . . .

My mother said, "He looks the way he did
thirty years ago, the day we got married,—
I'm *glad* I went;
I was afraid: now I can remember him
like that . . ."

Ruth, your last girlfriend, who wouldn't sleep with you
or marry, because you wanted her
to pay half the expenses, and "His drinking
almost drove me crazy—"
                        Ruth once saw you
staring into a mirror,
in your ubiquitous kerchief and cowboy hat,
say:
    "Why can't I look like a cowboy?"

You left a bag of money; and were
the unhappiest man
I have ever known well.

II

It's in many ways
a relief to have you dead.

                           I have more money.
Bakersfield is easier: life isn't so nude,
now that I no longer have to
face you each evening: mother is progressing
beautifully in therapy, I can almost convince myself
a good analyst would have saved you:

for I *need* to believe, as
always, that your pervasive sense of disappointment

proceeded from
trivial desires: but I fear
that beneath the wish to be a movie star,
cowboy, empire builder, all those
cheap desires, lay
radical disaffection
                         from the very possibilities
of human life . . .

Your wishes were too simple:
                    or too complex.

III

I find it difficult to imagine you
in bed, making love to a woman . . .

By common consensus, you were a *good* lover:
and yet,
mother once said: "Marriage would be better
if it weren't mixed up with sex . . ."

Just after the divorce,—when I was
about five,—I slept all night with you

in a motel, and again and again
you begged me
to beg her to come back . . .

I said nothing; but she went back
several times, again and again
you would go on a binge, there would be
another woman,
mother would leave . . .

You always said,
"Your mother is the only woman I've ever loved."

IV

Oh Shank, don't turn into the lies
of mere, neat poetry . . .

I've been reading Jung, and he says that we can
never get to the bottom
of what is, or was . . .

But *why* things were as they were
obsesses; I know that you
the necessity to contend with you
your *helplessness*
before yourself,
                    —has been at the center
of how I think my life . . .

                              And yet your voice, raw,
demanding, dissatisfied,
saying over the telephone:

        "How are all those bastards at Harvard?"

remains, challenging: beyond all the
patterns and paradigms
                    I use to silence and stop it.

V

I dreamed I *had* my wish:
                     —I seemed to see
the conditions of my life, upon
a luminous stage: how I could change,
how I could not: the root of necessity,
and choice.
           The stage was labelled
"Insight".
          The actors there
had no faces, I cannot remember
the patterns of their actions, but
simply by watching,

I knew that beneath my feet
the fixed stars
governing my life

had begun to fall, and melt . . .
                —Then your face appeared,

laughing at the simplicity of my wish.

VI

Almost every day
I take out the letter you wrote me in Paris.
. . . Why?

It was written
the year before you married Shirley; Myrtle,
your girlfriend, was an ally of mine
because she "took care of you,"
but you always
made it clear
she was too dumpy and crude to marry . . .

In some ways "elegant,"
with a pencil-thin, neatly clipped moustache,
chiselled, Roman nose, you were
a millionaire
and always pretended
you couldn't afford to go to Europe . . .

When I was a child,
you didn't seem to care if I existed.

Bakersfield, Calif
July 9, 1961

Dear Pinon.
    Sorry I haven't wrote to you sooner but glad to hear that you
are well and enjoying *Paris.*

I got your fathers day wire in the hospital where I put in about twelve days but I am very well now. I quit the ciggeretts but went through ten days of hell quitting and my back had been giving me hell.

It had been very hot here but the last few days has been very nice. Emily just got out of the hospital yesterday. She had her feet worked on. I guess she will tell you about it. Glad to hear you are learning some French.

We are just about through with potatoes. Crop was very good but no price at all whitch made it a poor year. Cattle are cheap too. It look like a bad year for all farmer's.

I don't know anything else to tell you. Take care of your self and enjoy it. Maybe you will never have another chance for another trip. I don't think I'll ever get the chance to go, so if you run into a extra special gal between 28 & 35 send her over here to me as all I know over here don't amount to mutch. Well I guess I'll close now as I am going over to see Emily.

Hoping to hear from you right away.

This address is 4019 Eton St. be sure and get it straight. Myrtle would like to know how much that watch amounts to. Let us know

Will close now and write soon.

Love 'Shank'

P.S. Excuse this writing as its about 30 years since I wrote a letter.

VII

How can I say this?
                        I think my psychiatrist
likes me: he knows
the most terrible things I've done, every stupidity,
inadequacy, awkwardness,
ignorance, the mad girl I screwed
because she once again and again
teased and rejected me, and whose psychic incompetence
I grimly greeted as an occasion for revenge;
he greets my voice

with an interest, and regard, and affection,
which seem to signal I'm worth love;

—you finally
forgave me for being your son, and in the nasty
shambles of your life, in which you had less and less
occasion for pride, you were proud
of me, the first Bidart
who ever got a B.A.; Harvard, despite
your distrust, was the crown;—but the way
you eyed me:
                        the *bewilderment*, unease:
the somehow always
tentative, suspended judgment . . .

—however *much* you tried (and, clearly,
you *did* try)
               you could not remake your
taste, and like me: could not remake
yourself, to give me

the grace
needed to look in a mirror, as I often can
now, with some equanimity . . .

VIII

When did I begin to substitute
insight, for prayer? . . .

                —You believed in neither:
but said, "My life is over,"
after you had married Shirley,
twenty-five years younger, with three
small children, the youngest
six months old; she was unfaithful
within two months, the marriage was simply
annulled . . .
           A diabetic, you didn't
take your insulin when you drank, and
almost managed to die
many times . . .
           You punished Ruth
when she went to Los Angeles for a weekend, by
beginning to drink; she would return home
either to find you in the hospital,
or in a coma on the floor . . .

                The exacerbation
of this seeming *necessity*
for connection—;
           you and mother taught me
there's little that's redemptive or useful
in natural affections . . .

I must *unlearn*; I must believe

you were merely a man—
with a character, and a past—;
                      you wore them,
                      unexamined,
like a nimbus of
furies

round your
greying, awesome head . . .

IX

What should I have done? In 1963,
you wanted to borrow ten thousand dollars
from me, so that we could buy cattle
together, under the name "Bidart and Son,"—
most of your money was tied up
in the increasingly noxious "Bidart Brothers,"
run by your brother, Johnny . . .

I said no,—
that I wanted to use the money
for graduate school; but I thought
if you went on a binge, and as had happened
before, simply threw it away . . .

The Bidarts agreed
you were *not* to be trusted; you accepted
my answer, with an air
of inevitability I was shocked at . . .

I didn't *want* to see your self-disgust;
—somehow, your self-congratulation
had eroded more deeply, much
more deeply, than even I had wished,—

but for *years*, how I had wished! . . .

I have a friend who says
that he has never felt a conflict
between something deeply wished or desired,
and what he thought was "moral" . . .

Father, such innocence
surely is a kind of *Eden*—; but,
somehow, I can't regret that we
are banished from that company—;
in the awareness, the
history of our contradictions and violence,
insofar as I am "moral" at all,
is the beginning of my moral being.

X

When I began this poem,
                              to see myself
as a piece of history, having a past
which shapes, and informs, and thus inevitably
limits—
              at first this seemed sufficient, the beginning of
freedom . . .
                    The way to approach freedom
was to acknowledge necessity:—
I sensed I had to become not merely
a speaker, the "eye," but a character . . .

And you had to become a character: with a past,
with a set of internal contradictions and necessities
which if I could *once* define, would at least
begin to release us from each other . . .

But, of course, no such knowledge is possible;—
as I touch your photographs, they stare back at me
with the dazzling, impenetrable, glitter of mere life . . .

You stand smiling, at the end of the twenties,
in a suit, and hat,
cane and spats, with a collie at your feet,
happy to be handsome, dashing, elegant:—

and though I cannot connect this image

with the end of your life, with the defensive
gnarled would-be cowboy,—

you seem happy at that fact, happy
to be surprising; unknowable; unpossessable . . .

You say it's what you always understood by freedom.

1968–69.

PART THREE

Vergil Aeneid *1.1-33*

Arms and the man I sing, the man and hero, who
driven by fate, by the gods' mere force and Juno's hate,
found Italy, found Latium, the man and hero
battered on land and sea, who founded our city,
brought us gods and lineage,
even to this, garlanded walls of substantial Rome.
     Muse, make me mindful of the causes, load upon me
knowledge of her sorrows, she whom men call the queen of the gods
but driven to drive the most earnest of men
to such misfortunes. After foundering Troy,
what human being would not have been satisfied?
     An ancient city, held by farmers, fronting Italy
and the mouth of the Tiber, then
magnificent in elegance, rich in courage:
such was Carthage—it is said, the city of Juno, and loved
by her even above Samos, seat of her shrine.
She wanted this new home of her weapons and chariot
first among men. But the fates did not so spin:
bathed in the faded pageant of Troy, in rue and despair,
a race was to come to rule over men,
merciless in war, graceful in victory.
She had heard that beloved Carthaginian Libya
would soon be a level plain.
Within her mind the resistless past returned:
scenes of burning Troy, herself as chief of destruction—
and deeper, to the causes in insult and wounded love
and proper mother's pride, Paris's
judgment, the bastard
founding of the city, Ganymede snatched above her own daughter:
out of this the Trojans must wander, must wander in error

seeking over the world's seas
what the remnant left by the Greeks and merciless Achilles
may never enjoy through the will of the queen of the gods:
how heavy the burden, to found the Roman race.

After Catullus

The day was calm . . . For the usual reason
I had gone into the country, and indeed
there seemed peace. Understanding friend:
with whom only
I can be frank; can even you
receive this as I received it?

I walked down into a field. The lions were in bloom,
crocus, hyacinth, coxcombs,
shouting to be so full of sun and seed.
I said to myself: "I must lie down."
They touched my face. I
could not see the sun.

In this darkness then: a sound became clear,
half-moaning
half-delight
of a girl—twelve?—lying
not five feet from me
with her legs spread apart. Above her in jeans

a boy maybe younger worked away . . . He was good!
But he didn't see me standing staring with blind eyes
in the sun. She resisted: his arms held her arms
firmly down
as the open front of his jeans disappeared
under her dress. I
put him to the sword!

With my prick.

To My Father

I walked into the room.
There were objects in the room. I thought I needed nothing
from them. They began to speak,
but the words were unintelligible, a painful cacophony . . .
Then I realized they were saying
                              the name
of the man who had chosen them, owned them,
ordered, arranged them, their deceased cause,
the secret pattern that made these things order.
I strained to hear: but
the sound remained unintelligible . . .
senselessly getting louder, urgent, deafening.

Hands over my ears, at last I knew
                              they would remain
inarticulate; your name was not in my language.

Another Life

*Peut-être n'es-tu pas suffisamment mort.
C'est ici la limite de notre domaine. De-
vant toi coule un fleuve.*

Valéry.

"—In a dream I never *exactly* dreamed,
but that is, somehow, the quintessence
of what I *might* have dreamed,

                Kennedy is in Paris

again; it's '61; once again
some new national life seems possible,
though desperately, I try to remain unduped,
even cynical . . .

            He's standing in an open car,

brilliantly lit, bright orange
next to a grey de Gaulle, and they stand
not far from me, slowly moving up the Champs-Elysées . . .

Bareheaded in the rain, he gives a short
choppy wave, smiling like a sun god.

—I stand and
look, suddenly at peace; once again mindlessly
moved,

       as they bear up the fields of Elysium

the possibility of Atlantic peace,

reconciliation between all that power, energy,
optimism,—

         and an older wisdom, without
illusions, without force, the austere source
of nihilism, corrupted only by its dream of Glory . . .

But no—; as I
watch, the style is

                    not quite right—;

               Kennedy is *too* orange . . .

And de Gaulle, white, dead
white, ghost white, not even grey . . .

                              As my heart
began to grieve for my own awkwardness and
ignorance, which would never be
soothed by the informing energies
                         of whatever
wisdom saves,—

               I saw a young man, almost
my twin, who had written
                    'MONSTER'
in awkward lettering with a crayon across
the front of his sweat shirt.
                    He was gnawing on his arm,

in rage and anger gouging up
pieces of flesh—; but as I moved to stop him, somehow
help him,
          suddenly he looked up,

and began, as I had, to look at Kennedy and de Gaulle:

and then abruptly, almost as if I were seeing him
through a camera lens, his figure
split in two,—
               or doubled,—

and all the fury
               drained from his stunned, exhausted face . . .

But only for a moment. Soon his eyes turned down
to the word on his chest. The two figures
again became one,

and with fresh energy he attacked the mutilated arm . . .

—Fascinated, I watched as this
pattern, this cycle,
                    repeated several times.

Then he reached out and touched me.

—Repelled,
            I pulled back . . . But he became
frantic, demanding that I become
the body he split into:
                    'It's harder
to manage *each* time! Please,
give me your energy;—*help me!*'

                              —I said it was impossible,
there was *no part* of us the same:
we were just watching a parade together:
(and then, as he reached for my face)
                              leave me *alone!*

He smirked, and said
I was never alone.

            I told him to go to hell.

He said that this was hell.

                              —I said it was impossible,
there was *no part* of us the same:
we were just watching a parade together:
                              when I saw

Grief, avenging Care, pale
Disease, Insanity, Age, and Fear,
                                —all the raging desolations

which I had come to learn were my patrimony;
the true progeny of my parents' marriage;
the gifts hidden within the mirror;

—standing guard at the gate of this place,
triumphant,
              striking poses
                          eloquent of the disasters they embodied . . .

—I took several steps to the right, and saw
Kennedy was paper-thin,
                        as was de Gaulle;
mere cardboard figures
whose possible real existence
lay buried beneath a million tumbling newspaper photographs . . .

—I turned, and turned, but now all that was left
was an enormous
                fresco;—on each side, the unreadable
                                fresco of my life . . .

The First Hour of the Night

(1990)

Now In Your Hand

1. Victor Hugo: Preface to *Les Misérables*, 1862

SO LONG AS, on this earth, in our civilization, fixed there by its laws and its customs, HELL EXISTS—A DAMNATION MADE BY MEN over and above the fate all men must face;

SO LONG AS the three great violations of our age,

> *men debased by the nature of their work*
> *women devoured by their hunger*
> *children stunted by night without light*

are unsolved, and even unseen;

SO LONG AS the world human beings have made is a world where we cannot breathe;

IN SUM, SO LONG AS ALL THAT IS AT HOME ON THIS EARTH ARE IGNORANCE AND MISERY WITHOUT RE-COURSE OR VOICE,

books such as the one now in your hand will not, I think, be, perhaps, useless.

2.

                        when

once, pursuing the enslaving enemies and enslaving protectors
of our civilization, but encountering
only the unthinkable, a blank screen, banal
interiority, commas multiplying ad infinitum, in
short, the appearance in his consciousness of the consciousness
of the appearance of himself

                        when he doubted he ever believed they ex

he found that they destroyed enemies and friends

using the means in which he believed,
this system in which in every sentence you can insert not

You remain . . .

You remain, bride whose recourse has been silence, and absence:—
you appear under the names *arena*, *stage*, but your essence

always is other and elsewhere, your gift
the voices of the dead filled and emptied by the future.

Protect against those who entering
the orifices of this house

seek to control it—

Muse, Autodidact, Collector,
renew its inmate dedicated to you.

By These Waters

What begins in recognition,—
. . . ends in obedience.

The boys who lie back, or stand up,
allowing their flies to be unzipped

however much they charge
however much they charge

give more than they get.

When the room went dark, the screen lit up.

By these waters on my knees I have wept.

Long and Short Lines

You who call me to weep afresh love's long since cancelled woe,—
. . . mock me

with you—

hypocrisy's thirst somewhere if you're anywhere must
now make you again pave someone's road to hell.

Toward that design cut long ago by your several divided nature
and mine,

. . . learn I too
twist, unchanged.

1989.

Book of Night

After the sun
fell below the horizon of the west,

THE SUN-GOD

(according to words carved
on the sarcophagus of the pharaoh Seti I)

each night, during the twelve hours of the night, must
journey through
THE WORLD THAT IS BENEATH THE WORLD, —
. . . must
meet, once again, the dead.

The hour that must follow the eleventh hour

is blank within my eye: —
I do not know what will make the sun rise again.

With a light placed
inside it, the sarcophagus carved out of alabaster

is transparent: —

here is the beginning of our night.

The First Hour of the Night

"This happened about twelve years before I died.

.

What I have to tell you

is the narrative of an evening and night, little more than
a succession of dreams, one
anxiety following another,—

the whole, somehow, for me (at least) *wound* and *balm*.

.

The friend I had been closest to throughout
my life, three years earlier, suddenly

was dead—;
            for three years, his son

had invited me to visit the family home,—
. . . the family 'seat,'

                a 'GREAT HOUSE'

inherited by my friend in his twenties at his
father's death, inherited now by his only son . . .

WHAT *USE* TO RETURN?—

During his life, both of us often insisted that our
philosophical discussions, ebullient
arguments, hydra-headed analyses of
the motivations, dilemmas that seemed to block
and fuel our lives,

                were central, crucial:—

but after his death, all I now could see

was the self-generating *logic* of his life, its distant,
inaccessible self-sufficiency . . .

He had been a storm at sea,—
. . . seen from land.

WHAT USE TO RETURN?

As I imagined standing again within that house,
—within that world he had been
given, but had so
transformed by his affections, curiosity, shifting
enthusiasms, care:—

walking up the central staircase, then, after
twenty feet, entering his study,—

. . . its obscure, *ARBITRARY*
FINALITY

stopped my breath.

—Three years (to the day) after this first death of
a friend my own age, his son

wrote that I would do his father's only child

a great kindness
if once again I came to stay, even for a night . . .

The house was (of course) changed.

. . . I suppose I had expected
a museum to my friend—;

instead, I found the embodiment of different interests,—
as well as incomprehension
of, or even the desire to ERASE, to BLUR

what in his father had seemed bold
or witty or coherent:—

an unsymmetrical, fragile Indonesian rocker
had been sold, because 'uncomfortable';—

curtains obscured the high bare rectangles of
windows whose light or blackness once
was shut out only by recessed, seldom-used shutters . . .

Half the books were stored,—
. . . or sold.

After dinner, we went into the study.

Neither of us sat in his father's chair.

Highbacked, winged, it still stood
at an angle, right of the fire,—and I sat

facing it, on
the left, where I had always sat . . .

The couch to my right was still there,—
he slumped at its far end.

The small coal fire, as always, burned one's face,—
. . . and failed to heat the dark, huge room.

—He put his hands to his temples, making
a kind of hood over his eyes;

I couldn't see his eyes.

Then he spoke:—
                    '. . . I can neither

SELL THIS HOUSE,—
nor LIVE IN IT.

                    If father had a favorite horse, you and I could

sacrifice and eat it
next to his grave—;

                    then set up its head on a stake

driven directly into the grave . . .

That's how Harva says the Tartars
convince the dead to STAY DEAD.

—They seldom succeed: if a dead man's
widow and children

                    GROW SICK

the shaman knows the dead are eating them . . .

You've known me since I was born—;

you know that I wasn't
waiting for father to die: I had my own

work, friends, income (I admit that I've always been
a spendthrift, but I wasted

my own money, not his—) . . .

The prerogatives that descended upon me at his death

—"position"; much more money; the freedom
implicit in the demands now
placed upon me—

I didn't connive, or even will: they came
in the course of things,—

             . . . *BECAUSE HE WAS NOT HERE.*

But I enjoy them; and even (now) expect them.

. . . *Again and again I dream*

             father has come back:—

he is standing in the hallway, as I
descend the staircase—;

he looks up at me, tired, relieved to be home . . .

He is whole: WELL: *NOT* changed,—
                    but even as I
rush down the steps to *EMBRACE* him

(even as the irreparable
FACT that drained and diminished the world

ISN'T fact,—)

I know that I don't

          want him to have come back:—

all this is HIS, not MINE—; I AM
AGAIN WHAT HIS DEATH MADE ME NO LONGER . . .

Before I reach him, an elated circle of
servants and friends

surrounds him,—
                    and leads him off . . .

As they disappear, his head turns
back to look at me.

—Then I know that each object that father
chose for this house but
                    ABSENT now from it

says that everything ever unresolved
clearly FOREVER
                    is unresolvable between us—;

for though I *must* give it all back, I
CAN'T give it all back,—

I've already

                    spent too much money!—

. . . thus, though I know that no creature
possesses anything on this earth,

sweating I wake up
terrified that father has returned to it:—

BAFFLED,—
                    and APPALLED,—

to find that what I want is his death . . .'

Then he stopped.

There was a long silence.

The voice I heard as he said all this

—in a sudden
intonation, a passing phrase, in the pervasive
self-wounding relentlessness of its logic,—

was his *father's* . . .

The FIST at the center of my chest
REFUSED TO UNCLENCH

until he and I, the furniture we
sat on, the room, the house,
THE VERY WORLD ITSELF

cracked apart,

then SELF-COMBUSTED,—

. . . *self-consumed by our own self-contradictions.*

I told him that when I was a child I had a pony

who was, for a period, my
life—;

. . . even now,—if I close
my eyes, and look into his face

I am a boy again, looking into the face of a neurasthenic
panicked *mute* creature like himself—;
in SECRET

ALLIANCE forged
half-against what we lacked:—

               WORDS, a world that demonstrated its

mastery over us
by coercive involuted adult human speech . . .

He was a high-strung, intelligent miniature colt,
my size:—
        . . . the prize of my sixth birthday.

Perhaps time and retrospect have improved our mutual absolute
trust, delight, connection:—

but this was the first of those passionate
attachments, passionate
JUDGMENTS that *here* 'like-*ANSWERS*-like,'

'*SOUL*-answers-*SOUL*,'

             which since my childhood,—

whether in relation to animal, FRIEND,
an artist or performer I've discovered, or work of art,—

(—except where feeling has been
bewildered by the desire

for the *RECIPROCATION* of *EROTIC* DESIRE,—)

have never betrayed me: never when I have
encountered again in body or memory

WHAT I LOVED

seemed then stupid, ill-
founded, grounded merely in willfulness,
               MORE ILLUSION . . .

At nine, I was sent to boarding school.

The approach of this cataclysm held no allure for me,
rather I felt rage and a sense of betrayal—;

but in fact, within a few weeks

books, the desire to dominate the attention of
my teachers,
                    and even wary camaraderie with my peers

for the first time,
                    SWALLOWED ME . . .

When I, UNWILLINGLY, arrived home on our first
holidays, I was told that several horses

had come down with a fever,
                    including mine,—

. . . *that my horse was dying.*

The next day he was carted off.

                    THERE WAS NO GRAVE.

Perhaps my earliest memory that is absolutely
fixed in scene and time

is the black horse flies big as thumbs
covering and clinging to his body—; the weird unseasonable

blood-red sunset saturating the world

while I *knew* his body was being carried off but
HOWLING I was *HELD BACK* within the house . . .

—Much later, when I was twelve, thirteen, fourteen,
in my dreams

        my little horse again and again

came back—;

he wanted to play, for me once again to mount
him and ride,—

but I had no time, what I now was
interested in were friends, school, my studies:—

. . . besides, as I stood
next to him,

        HE WAS TOO SMALL —;

I had grown, and he was now
TOO SMALL to ride—;

        with a shiver, a stamp and sound
of torment, he seemed to take this in . . .

I told my friend's son that what he had felt
in his dream

        was nothing so simple as GREED
or SELFISHNESS—;

        that later, in my thirties,
again I had known very similar emotions

after other deaths—;

        THAT THERE SEEMED TO BE SOMETHING
STRUCTURAL IN HUMAN RELATIONS

MAKING WHAT WE HAD FELT

—well, *'IMPERSONAL'* . . .

Though he thanked me for my generosity and
candor, and said that he felt

not only exhausted but somewhat better,—
. . . as I mounted the stairs to my room that night

what I felt
was woe, unameliorated, unappeased.

•

Now follows my

'DREAM OF THE HISTORY OF PHILOSOPHY,'—

. . . for that night, in my room, as I threw
off my clothes, seeking in sleep only
oblivion, erasure of the throbbing but
irremediably ignorant *I*,

—angry at I did *NOT* know what,—

above my bed I saw, again,
what since my
first visit had hung there,

Volpato's fine
etching of Raphael's

'SCHOOL OF ATHENS' . . .

I remembered, with a sudden and flooding
access of pleasure, the first time I had seen, in

Rome, Raphael's fresco:—

here, under the image of the many-breasted
GODDESS OF PHILOSOPHY

                (in a medallion in the ceiling)

flanked by two angels
announcing

        'KNOWLEDGE OF THE CAUSES OF THINGS,'—

. . . at the center of the high arch of the fresco itself,

framed there by a vast, symmetrical,
seemingly stable but
essentially (at least according to
some writers) unbuildable architecture,—

. . . their two heads isolated by three great
descending central arches
that, dreamlike, open to the sky,—

. . . calmly presiding over an 'ideal' assembly of the great
philosophers of Antiquity

             (not only metaphysicians and
scientists, but students, a soldier,
the leaning, listening figure of
Averroës, commentator, representative of Islam,—)

PLATO and ARISTOTLE

        by their *PARALLEL* but *OPPOSITE*

gestures (Aristotle
pointing downward, Plato upward,—)

             DIVIDE and ORDER

this debating, brooding, teaching, writing, nearly
disharmonious multitude

(on the side of Aristotle, representatives of the 'exact'
sciences: Euclid, Ptolemy—;
                                    with 'speculative'
thinkers—Heraclitus, Pythagoras—on the side of Plato)

. . . *opposite* gestures that, *JANUS-LIKE*, show
us where to seek the causes of things.

In this 'ideal' COMMUNITY OF THE SPIRIT,

—the social world as the social world
never is,—

            DEATH, RAGE, and EROS

have receded to adorn recesses in the architecture:—

. . . on the left, under a yielding, even
voluptuous APOLLO holding his lyre,

an aging Triton
seizes the breast of a resisting Sea Nymph—;

. . . on the right, Medusa's severed
face, mouth frozen open in an *O* of horror,

from ATHENA'S victorious shield stares
powerless:—
            ATHENA, Goddess of WISDOM, protector of

the *Home, Family, Reason, Civilization* . . .

When I first saw this scene (—the title
'*SCHOOL* of *ATHENS*' a misapprehension

imposed on it in the Eighteenth Century,—)

I was largely ignorant of the intricate
iconography
        connecting the room's four walls and ceiling:—

'PHILOSOPHY' looks across at 'THEOLOGY,'
                while 'POETRY'

faces 'JURISPRUDENCE,'—each

itself divided: 'Canon
Law' and 'Civil Law' . . .

—In the interrelations and elegant
distinctions informing its walls and ceiling,
this is a compendium, even synthesis of

Renaissance speculative, religious, aesthetic thinking:—

an 'ideal' Renaissance TEMPLE OF THE HUMAN MIND . . .

Its *PREMISE*,—

        the Neo-Platonic Christian-Humanist
CONFIDENCE that the world's obdurate
contradictions, terrifying
unintelligibility,

        can be *tamed* by CLASSIFICATION,—

. . . Time
now has effaced.

This room,—
        intended as the site of the Pope's personal

library, then where he signed, before assembled
dignitaries of the highest Papal
tribunal, bulls and official documents,—

was the first of the rooms that Raphael
painted for the Pope:—

                              only twenty-five, with
little reputation, he had been summoned from
Florence to Rome at the suggestion of his

patron, Bramante,
                    architect of the new *St. Peter's* . . .

Decoration of the room was already begun,—

. . . but no one is certain how much
Sodoma, six years Raphael's senior, had completed:—

for when the Pope saw Raphael's sketches

(*there is never enough wall space
here, at the CENTER of POWER,*—)

. he ordered everything that Sodoma had painted destroyed.

In the fresco, next to Raphael's own
self-portrait, is the face of
                              Sodoma—;

both stand behind Euclid (Geometry is
central to the painter's skill at perspective,—)

'Euclid' has the head of Bramante . . .

Raphael, without
illusions, looks out at us—;

                    Sodoma
smiles,—

        without rancor, or humiliation,
absorbed in the conversation before him . . .

In this 'ideal' COMMUNITY OF THE SPIRIT,

Socrates and Aristotle are modelled on
Antique busts, but Plato

has the features of Leonardo:—

Heraclitus (self-enclosed but
writing), the short, hooded, stonecutter's

smock of a *pensieroso*
                    Michelangelo . . .

'*The APOLLO who*
            SHARES REIGN
                        with ATHENA here

is the God, not of Reason, but POETRY,—'

I said to myself as I began to fall asleep;—
and then,

fixing the arc of the fresco before my mind:—

'*Here,*—*EVERYONE feels it,*—
the GESTURE OF PLATO and the GESTURE OF ARISTOTLE

are ONE . . .'

Knowing that I loved it, my friend once had
placed the 'School of Athens'

above my bed.—

Smiling, now I remembered this—; *'Now I
must sleep . . .'* Then, to my

humiliation and shame,

I was *IN* it,—

that tumultuous, PERISHED world (now
NOT PERISHED,—)

lay before me:—

out of estrangement I had gained or been given
entrance: privilege

in *no way* EARNED,—

above me, past the Temple's
multitudinous, strangely empty rising steps,

Ptolemy still
held aloft the green-and-blue *GLOBE* OF THE *EARTH*:—

then
        (—as I turned to crouch
or hide,—)
                from the distance on either side I saw

a long row of men, dressed in the varied garments of
succeeding centuries,

            approach the steps where I stood.

—When each figure
passed me, for a moment looking into my eyes
full-face,
            I tried to recognize him:—

there
            (—*just as I had imagined them in the light of*
their portraits, —)

                        was BRUNO, one button missing

on his long black scholar's gown, still
smelling of sulphur from the fires of the Inquisition, —

he held a book titled
                        '*FEAST OF ASHES*' —;

                                        DESCARTES, —

priestlike in devotion to his self-made
revolution, —
                . . . HEAVY-LIDDED, as if worn out by
thought, or lessons at dawn for the Queen of Sweden —;

HEGEL and SCHELLING,
                        walking hand-in-hand, —

                                        as in the morning of
their young
COLLABORATION, before distance, fame, silence —;

. . . these, and so many others
                        (—*each*

alive as his voice on the page : —

each body now inseparable from its
fate, yet with the unachieved
                        purposeful will of the living, —)

ascended the steps, and,
                        WITHOUT
BARRIER,
            began to listen and mix and speak

in earnest debate, yet strangers' courteous deference,
with the philosophers of Antiquity . . .

Irrational *HAPPINESS* seized me:—

not at the absence of discord (discord
will come)
         but to see

this that at last lies before
me is as I have known real—;

after chimeras of CONTINGENCY and resistless
SELF-ESTRANGEMENT,—

. . . to see chimeras of the real.

Then, something happened which I did
NOT expect
         even in a dream—;

. . . as if compelled or drawn by inner
necessity, DIVIDING they rushed to join themselves

into GROUPS:—
         groups that, now, I saw

had been there, though I had never seen them

(—but my words are mere
SUMMARY, for what I remembered when I

woke, seemed the faithless shadow of what I had seen) . . .

First the movement pressed to the right, where
next to Ptolemy (wearing on his gown a resplendent
globe of the heavens,—)
         Archimedes

leaning down to the stone beneath them drew his circles—;

. . . here, around these
two figures,

        gathered *Materialists, Mathematical
Naturalists, Positivists*

                (I recognized Hobbes—; Comte
arguing with Descartes—; then, restlessly
circling at the edges of the group, D'Alembert
                        whose ironic smile

seemed to mock the dreams of the metaphysicians,—)

. . . all those thinkers who see
within the indecipherable, furious
cataract of life, within bewildering, annihilating

flux, a great *intelligible* PROCESS:—

measurable, universal N A T U R E,—
                    impartial,

non-censorious, whose unbreakable Chain
of unvarying, coherent Laws

frees us from the prison-house of human
superstition, religious dogma, hallucination . . .

Here MIND and CONSCIOUSNESS

                are *BODY*—;

'free-will,'—
        . . . DARKNESS still-undispelled by Science.

Now Comte,—
                    systematizer of
Positivism, standing as if confident that he

is HEIR to the immense authority (. . . confirming
its insight into REALITY,—)

conferred on Science by its transformation of the world,—

announces to devoted, listening
thinkers from all nations
                              (his face flushed, eyes
shrewd but credulous)

A *NEW* CLERGY: a scientific-industrial
elite henceforth translating to
                              expectant, hungry Society

'invariable laws' new-found by fecund Science . . .

—As he spoke, Descartes
                              (abruptly once again the French
cavalier, setting forth with bold stride,—)

disengaged himself from all these figures,—

                                        turning his gaze
irresistibly toward
the center of the Temple, to a *second* GROUP, which had

assembled, arranged itself as if magnetized
around SOCRATES as its center:—

                              with an old, god-like Plato and
young
Aristotle each writing down his words at his feet . . .

Here the conviction that
MIND, SPIRIT, CONSCIOUSNESS

are merely ar

INTERPOLATION
in the immense text of the physical universe

was *reversed*—;
as Socrates spoke

(among those listening I saw
Plotinus—; Cicero—; Christian
theologians: Augustine held
the *Confessions,* Thomas Aquinas distractedly
fingered strands of straw from a crown of straw on his head,—)

as he explained that through *DIALECTIC*,

dialogue, argument by

CONTRADICTION proceeding to the *reconciliation* of
contradiction (for only contradiction impels
thought, and what is thought

but the silently-occurring internal dialogue
of the soul with itself?—)

(. . . pugnosed and pugnacious, Socrates
yet made me feel that he had seen in
spirit, what he struggled to express in words,—)

as he explained that through *DIALECTIC*, our
power of REASON,

we can make our way to an order
past the delusions of custom, self-deception, desire,—

. . . and can then, by an act of
CHOICE,

CHANGE,—*CORRECT* our lives:—

suddenly, from behind
his voice, blending with his voice,

was a woman's voice:—

(I moved slightly to the left, to see
its source,—)

. . . there, with the seated figures of Dante
and Sappho (who grasped disintegrating
pages of a book in her hand)
                              rapt, silent before her,

was S H E H E R E Z A D E:—

                              (seated on an embroidered
pillow, wearing transparent
silks, plucking an instrument)

whose wizard songs
                    (I have known them since
my youth)
           beguile the SWORD that hangs above her . . .

Troubled, excited voices
soon broke my attention—;
                              turning back, I saw

the circle of listeners now had divided
into disputing factions,—

                              while Augustine, standing to one side,
stared out at them . . .

—What one thinker confidently
ASSERTED,
           another *spurned* as ILLUSION—;

what one human being
flew from, another sought—;

some struggled to reconcile the wisdom of
Greece
          with Christ's revelation,—

. . . while other, melancholy voices
doubted the free sufficient autonomy of

REASON and the HUMAN WILL

faced with our confusion, weak and isolated
organs of perception, helplessness . . .

The abrupt arrival of Descartes

                              (for the first time, I noticed
that the hair thickly
growing beneath his lower lip,
                              on one
side, was *shaved off*,—)

                    then, later, of the stooped,

slightly built Kant, with his cane
and three-cornered hat, his features
hardened as if by the strain of thought,

brought brief ORDER to this spectacle—;

                              . . . but Augustine,

pushing past all this with a gesture of
REVULSION that seemed to rise from
an intuition indistinguishable from himself,

—his hands now
empty,—

       already had abandoned the scene before him,
                                       turning to

a third, *final* GROUP, gathered at
the left of the temple, whose center

was PYTHAGORAS and HERACLITUS . . .

From this milling, mercurial crowd
                       (—Hegel now
looked at one moment like
Bismarck, at another like Shelley,—)

words emerge:—

           *MASTER AND
SLAVE. Predestination. Preservation of
the Species. GOD IMMANENT IN
NATURE. Race. Blood. STAGES OF ABSOLUTE
MIND. Progress. Class. The inexorable laws of
History, the Psyche, the Age.—*
                     *LOGOS. THE WORLD
AS WILL AND IDEA. THE ONE.—*
                     *The inescapable society of
the dead and the living, who
have made us what we are . . .*

Here the Materialists have been, as it were,
turned on their heads:—

now S P I R I T,—

         immanent, transcendant, or unknowable,—

is *ground* of BODY, *governs* BODY:—

. . . the single human psyche
powerless within the immeasurable

     power of its *LAWS, GOALS, WILL* . . .

Reached by daring to contemplate in a calm spirit
COHERENCE (or by hard, practiced
submission)

   'freedom' here is to *accept* NECESSITY—;

or else, when intolerable existence
wholly becomes the snake that swallows its own
tail,—

   . . . *TO SMASH THE HEAD OF THE SNAKE.*

Here ceaseless human
choices, decisions, dilemmas,
     MORTALITY itself,

is ILLUSION:—
    the cunning used upon
us to silence the voice
within that says:—

   Someone else
led my life. I am an ONLOOKER ON MY OWN LIFE . . .

—Then, among those listening to
Schopenhauer,

   I saw my dead friend—;

I am *CERTAIN* that I saw him, though

when I approached him, standing
just behind him,—
    when he
turned at my touch,—

his head was a C L O U D
dispersed into discrete
atoms—;

as if I had drawn too close to a painting made
out of discrete spots of separate color,

HE was no longer THERE—;

(. . . inheritor inheriting
inheritors, he had worked to transform an inheritance

transformed in its
turn:—
as if the SOUL,

delivered over unconscious and defenseless
not only to this world of

THINGS, but to its own DARKNESS,—

. . . flinging itself into the compensations that the world
and its own self

offer it, but finding the light of SELF-KNOWLEDGE

only through MEDIATION,

through WORKS and SIGNS,—

seeing and remaking itself within
that broken mirror made

by all the things that it has inherited
and remade,—

. . . in the end,

ALIENATES its Being in them:—)

the spectral E M P T I N E S S became only
emptier before me

as I advanced toward him,—

. . . until at last, surrounded by
nothing, with resignation

turning I drew back—;
                            not before

Augustine, engaged in animated argument
with Spinoza and Bruno, was EMBRACED

by Luther: appalled, recoiling,
he fled . . .

                      .

Now, as I lay
dreaming in the house of my dead friend,

finally I saw the THREE GROUPS
in one view:—

                I was exhausted, I wanted to
STOP, at last to have reached BOTTOM—;

. . . but busy figures ceaselessly rushed
between the groups, trying to MEDIATE:—
                                    for all these

conflicting intuitions surely were
grounded in the nature of the universe,—

in the relationship between the impenetrable, immeasurable
UNIVERSE that lies WITHIN as well as beyond us

and the solitary, finite perceiving mind,—

. . . indeed, I felt
pain at this scene:—to see

PHILOSOPHY itself

divided, torn
                into three, or even *more* directions—;

. . . the unity of my being
torn, for I had felt RECOGNITION

before the TRUTH that united *each* GROUP in its turn—;

but as I strove for
UNITY OF THOUGHT, in vain the mediators hastened
to and fro among the groups:—

. . . now a hostile alienation
envelops them, the distance between them

increases, the ground DISAPPEARS
beneath their bewildered, desperate feet . . .

The Temple itself, then, collapsed:—
                                . . . as the ground

engulfed, SWALLOWED all that I
had seen,

(—this *'tradition'* that I cannot
THINK MY LIFE

without, nor POSSESS IT within—;)

the frozen facial mask of
                Medusa, hung on Athena's shield, suddenly

SMILED,—

     . . . *SMIRKED.*

Then, I wanted to shout at this
destruction, this RUIN, not only in

pain, but in relief:—

       Whenever human beings have felt
CONVICTION that what they possess is indeed

'KNOWLEDGE OF THE CAUSES OF THINGS,'—

. . . whenever this conviction has been shared by, animated
a whole society, or significant
group within society,—

the ancient hegemony of POWER and PRIESTHOOD
is reconstituted—;

      implicit within each
vision of CAUSE, a structure of POWER:—

          an imagination not only of ·
where power resides, but SHOULD, MUST reside—;

. . . At the end of the First Crusade,
        when their goal
JERUSALEM
     fell at last before the Crusaders,

Christian troops running through the streets
stabbed, mutilated, slew
      everyone they saw—;

the savagery of the massacre
perhaps UNEXAMPLED (these
facts, I assure you, a matter of record,—)

in the history of Wars fought mainly for *Gain* or *Glory*:—

. . . in the narrow lanes, rivers of blood carrying headless
bodies and fragments of bodies

reached the horses' hocks—;

the Jewish community, huddling for safety in
the central synagogue,
                        was barricaded

in by the Crusaders, and burnt alive—;

after two days,—
                when,
gone like snow on the lawn in a hot sun,
the frenzy of RIGHTEOUS ANGER and REVENGE
had passed,—

               the few thousand still
alive from a population that before numbered forty thousand

were assembled
near the gates, and sold as slaves . . .

—Damascus and Baghdad
were shocked at the fate of the Holy City:—
                            vowing

RECOMPENSE . . .

The *'moral law within'*

                       (for Kant, the ground
of the moral life itself, *CERTAIN, BEAUTIFUL, FIXED*
like the processional of stars above our heads,—)

is near to MADNESS—; everything terrible
but buried in human motivation

released, justified

by SELF-RIGHTEOUSNESS and FANATICISM—;

. . . then, as I struggled to find words
to *punish*

confidence in the possession of truth,

I had the sick sensation of
falling, the stones
were cracking, giving way beneath my feet, and

suddenly, *AT THE SAME TIME*,

I knew that nothing that I,—*HEIR
TO THE AGES,*—

might reach or understand or grasp

will lodge safe
in *unhistorical* existence—; SAFE

within the hungry blankness of a culture *WITHOUT
WISDOM*, its wisdom the negative
wisdom embraced by exhaustion after
centuries of the Wars of Religion . . .

.

Thus, infected with the desolation of
HISTORY's

leprosy,—*LEPROSY* of SPIRIT,—

the stones

breaking, disappearing as my working legs
flailed in air,—

I woke.

Despair was what I felt.

At last, after fitful, thrashing

sleeplessness, again I slept, and for
a final time that night,
                    dreamt:—

. . . a brown, wide, desolate, broken only by
scars and protuberances, DUN landscape

stretched without boundary before me.

Then, STOOPING, staring out into this
barrenness,

I realized that on my back I was carrying

—*HAD* carried
all my life,—

          the *ENTRAILS* of my horse—;

secret, familiar
weight, either chosen or thrust upon me too long ago

now to put down, or often remember . . .

What at one moment looked parched, dun, desolate,
the next moment was
                    ochre, glowing, burnished—;

as I walked, what first had seemed
scars, as if the earth were WOUNDED too

deeply to heal without visible
mark, now I saw

were deep *pits* dug by men and women who
slowly carried
                    the earth dug

out of the pits, heaping it up to make
the hill next to each hole.

                Other women and men filled in

other pits, leveling these hills . . .

Two SIGNS stood against the horizon:—

        THE GREAT ACT OF BURYING

        THE GREAT ACT OF DIGGING UP

Because these human beings seemed concentrated, ABSORBED
—at moments anxious, even
tormented, at others earnest, eager
as if
      ANSWERING THEIR NATURE,—

. . . I could not tell whether this work was
freedom, or servitude.

Then, suddenly entangling my feet were
dozens of just-born
              LAMBS, stretching their necks to reach their

mothers next to them:—

hungry, SUCKING mouths stretched toward
swollen, distended udders that I saw must be

painful *unless* sucked—;

. . . *RECIPROCITY*,—
           I thought,—
                  not the chick within
the egg, who by eating its way
out, must DESTROY the egg to become itself . . .

Then, as I reached to steady the ENTRAILS
on my back,
                    I bent down to watch more closely:—

. . . hypnotized, I saw eager lambs
                              suck the paps of an

at-one-moment
YIELDING, relieved, even voluptuously
satisfied, but at-the-next-moment
sleepy, withdrawing, now
                    INDIFFERENT, *hostile* NATURE . . .

I felt again that
PENETRATION OF KNOWLEDGE that is almost like

illness, an invading sickness:—

. . . envious, yet afraid of
getting kicked in the head, I wanted

to lie against a ewe's
breathing, sleeping side . . .

—When at last both ewes and lambs
slept,
          I walked to the edge of a pit:—

. . . there, standing
at the bottom, looking up at me,

                              was my little horse—;

I was *afraid*: had he FORGIVEN what must have seemed
to him, unfaithfulness?

                    —*WAS* UNFAITHFULNESS?—

I worked my way down the steep, loose,
yielding sides of the pit.

When I reached bottom, as I lay his
ENTRAILS before him,
                    I saw that they had become

MY COLOR,
                    after years of carrying them:—

. . . slowly, he bent down his
head, sniffed, then

                    ATE THE ENTRAILS—;

expectant, he
looked up at me:—

as I climbed on
his back, startled once again by his
animal warmth as I clung to him,
                              —now

somehow *NEITHER*
NOT THE SAME SIZE, NOR THE SAME SIZE,—

we rose out of the pit,—

                    . . . and I
woke—;

. . . though I had no impulse to relate this dream to
the categories and Figures dreamt earlier,—

though I had no evidence whether it issued from
the Gate of IVORY or the Gate of HORN,—

(from which Gate *true* dreams come, and which
FALSE, frankly

I've never been able to remember,—)

as I retell it, the ASHHEAP begins to GLOW AGAIN—;

. . . for I woke
with a sense of

beneficence:—

an emotion which, though it did *not*
erase, TRANSFORMED

what earlier had overwhelmed
consciousness lying SLEEPLESS between dream and dream."

•

This is the end of the first hour of the night.

Appendix

An Interview—With Mark Halliday (1983)

Halliday: When I think about your two books, and the poems that I know will be in your third book, I seem to see a movement away from autobiographical material toward poems in which the characters are distinct from yourself—Nijinsky, Ellen West. Do you see a "story" of your choice of subjects for poems as beginning in family and autobiography and moving to something else? And if so, why has that happened?

Bidart: I've made a list of the subjects I hope we'll be able to take up in this interview: prosody; voice; "action"; punctuation; the relation of "personal" (or autobiographical) and "impersonal" elements in a poem; the struggle to make life *show* itself in a work of art.

It's hard to talk about any one of these things without talking about all of them—in my work at least, they seem to me so tangled, inextricable.

The heart of my first book was, as you say, autobiographical; but the story of how I came to this subject matter as the *necessary* subject matter for me at that time is bound up with discovering a prosody, figuring out (among other things) how to write down, how to "fasten to the page" the voice—and movements of the voice —in my head.

I wrote a lot of poems before the poems in my first book, *Golden State,* but they were terrible; no good at all. I was doing what many people start out by doing, trying to be "universal" by making the entire poem out of assertions and generalizations about the world —with a very thin sense of a complicated, surprising, opaque world outside myself that resisted the patterns I was asserting. These generalizations, shorn of much experience, were pretty simple-minded and banal.

Nonetheless, though the poems were thin, I was aware that what I heard, the rhythms and tones of voice in my head, I didn't know how to set down on paper. When I set the words down in the most "normal" ways, in terms of line breaks and punctuation, they didn't at all look to the eye the way I heard them in my head.

Halliday: Can you give an example from any of these poems?

Bidart: I remember a poem which ended with a sentence from Samuel Johnson, "The mind can only repose on the stability of truth." As I heard this sentence, it had a weight and grimness, a large finality it just didn't have as I first typed it. In the attempt to *make* this sentence look the way I heard it, I typed the words hundreds of different ways, with different punctuation and line breaks, for weeks. And I never did get them right; in the end, I realized the poem wasn't any good in the first place.

I never had a romance with writing *verse.* What caught me about writing poems was not the fascination of using meter and rhyme—I knew somehow, however gropingly and blindly, that there must be some way to get down the motions of the voice in my head, that somehow the way to do this was to write in *lines.* Lines, not only sentences or paragraphs. When I tried to "translate" the phrases in my head into formal metrical or rhymed structures, they went dead. It seemed that my own speech just wasn't, as so much English has always been, basically iambic. (There are lines of pentameter in my poems, but usually they represent some order or "plateau" of feeling I'm moving toward, or moving away from.)

What I *was* in love with was the possibility of bringing together many different kinds of thing in a poem. When I was an undergraduate, Eliot was probably my favorite (twentieth-century) poet; but Pound was the more liberating. *The Cantos* are very brilliant and they're also obviously very frustrating and in some ways, I guess, a mess. But they were tremendously liberating in the way that they say that anything can be gotten into a poem, that it doesn't have to change its essential identity to enter the poem—if you can create a structure that is large enough or strong enough, *anything* can retain its own identity and find its place there. *Four Quartets* is more perfect, but in a way its very perfection doesn't open up new aesthetic possibilities—at least it didn't for me then. *The Cantos,* and Pound's work as a whole, did; and do.

Halliday: As an undergraduate, did you already think of yourself as a poet?

Bidart: I *wanted* to be a poet as far back as I can remember, but I didn't think I could be. In college, many of my friends were far more fluent than I; they really knew how to shape something eloquently into a poem. My poems were always (with, maybe, one exception) awkward, bony, underwritten. My poems had vast structures of meaning and symbol, and about three words on the page.

Halliday: Could we go back now to your discovery of what you did have to do—the transition from those too abstract poems that were not successful, toward whatever it was that made you able to write the poems in *Golden State.* Could you talk about your years of graduate school, what you were reading and what you were thinking about, what you wanted to do?

Bidart: Really to answer that question I have to go back much further, because it's all bound up with wanting to be an artist when I was very young, and the different ways I imagined being an artist as I grew up.

When I was a kid, I was crazy about movies. In Bakersfield, I think movies were the most accessible art form, in terms of new things happening and being done in the arts—I mean, we didn't have the New York City Ballet or a great symphony orchestra, we didn't have a season of plays. But we did have, each week, surrounded by publicity, glamour and controversy, these incredibly interesting movies. As early as I can remember, I wanted to be an artist; I certainly knew I didn't want to be a farmer, as my father was. Briefly, I imagined becoming an actor; but very quickly it was clear to me that the person who really *made* movies was the director. By the time I was in high school, I was determined somehow to become a director. I thought a lot, read a lot about movies; I graduated from fan magazines, to reviews of contemporary films, to books like Paul Rotha's *The Film Till Now*. Because, in Bakersfield in high school, I could actually *see* almost none of the "serious," "art" films I was reading about, I ferociously held a great many opinions about things I had never experienced—the faith, for example, that the coming of sound had been a disaster to film as an art.

So, in college, I was determined to become a film director, and a *serious* film director. I wanted films to be as ambitious and complex as the greatest works of art—as Milton, Eliot, Joyce. I thought, at first, that I might become a philosophy major; but in the desolation of positivism and analytic linguistic skepticism that dominated American academic philosophy in the fifties, it seemed that the moral and metaphysical issues that had traditionally been the world, the province of philosophy, had been taken over by literature. *Ulysses* and *Absalom, Absalom!* and Yeats' "The Tower" seemed closer to Plato and Aristotle than what academic philosophers then were doing. One of my teachers at the University of California, Riverside, where I was an undergraduate, was a marvelous exception to this—Philip Wheelwright, who had written about literature and aesthetics, as well as translated Aristotle, Heraclitus. I was an earnest and clumsy freshman, and he was wonderfully humane and generous. (The first time I ever heard Maria Callas was in his living room, when he played to a final meeting of a class excerpts from her second recording of *Lucia*. I remember he was upset because he felt that it wasn't, compared to her first recording, nearly as well sung.)

Halliday: So you became an English major?

Bidart: I became an English major. Of course it's impossible to recapitulate all—or even the central—intellectual and emotional dramas of those years. But two books I particularly loved are relevant here.

First, Trilling's *The Liberal Imagination*: Trilling's sense, in "The Meaning of a Literary Idea," that one doesn't have to share "belief" in an author's "ideas," but has to feel their cogency, that the *activity* on the author's part has to be in a satisfying relation to the difficulty, the density of his materials. In "Art and Fortune," there is a long passage of great eloquence about "the beautiful circuit of thought and desire" (James' phrase), which culminates in this sentence:

> The novel has had a long dream of virtue in which the will, while never abating its strength and activity, learns to refuse to exercise itself upon the unworthy objects with which the social world tempts it, and either conceives its own right objects or becomes content with its own sense of its potential force —which is why so many novels give us, before their end, some representation, often crude enough, of the will unbroken but in stasis.

This image of the will "unbroken but in stasis"—after having "exhausted all that part of itself which naturally turns to the inferior objects offered by the social world"—and which has therefore "learned to refuse" . . . This image has haunted me: it seems to me a profound pattern, one of the central, significant actions that many works have, in different ways with different implications, *felt as necessary*. The passage also taught me, I think, one way a work of art can conclude without concluding—how it can reach a sense of "resolution," or completion, without "resolving" things that are inherently unresolvable. In college, I read these pages so many times I find I've almost memorized them.

The notion of "action" in Francis Fergusson's *The Idea of a Theater* is crucial to my understanding of poetry (and of writing in general)—so crucial, that I want to get polemical about it. Its source, of course, is Aristotle's *Poetics,* the statement that "tragedy is the imitation of an action." Fergusson cites Kenneth Burke on "language as symbolic action," and quotes Coleridge: unity of action, Coleridge says, "is not properly a rule, but in itself the great end, not only of the drama, but of the epic, lyric, even to the candle-flame of an epigram—not only of poetry, but of poesy in general, as the proper generic term inclusive of all the fine arts."

But the sense that a poem must be animated by a unifying, central action—that it both "imitates" an action and is *itself* an action—has been largely ignored by twentieth-century aesthetics. It was never an animating idea in the poetics of modernism. That doesn't mean that poets have ignored it in practice. When Pound, for example, writes that he has "schooled" himself "to write an epic poem which begins 'In the Dark Forest,' crosses the Purgatory of human error, and ends in the light," he is describing, of course, an action—a journey undertaken and suffered by the central consciousness of his poem, a journey that begins somewhere, goes somewhere, ends somewhere, a journey the *shape* of which has significance. But though Pound's poem was intended to imitate this action, the action that the actual poem he wrote inscribes is, we now all know, quite different. Its shape is tragic, and far more painful.

The notion that a poem imitates an action, and *is* an action, seems to me so necessary now because it helps free poetry from so many dead ends—"good description," the mere notation of sensibility, "good images," "good lines," or mere wit. Let me emphasize that an "action" is *not* a "moral," or merely something intended that the poet cold-bloodedly executes. Like Pound, a poet may *intend* that the action have a certain shape: but (again like Pound) any writer who is serious, as he moves through his materials, will inevitably find that what his poem must enact, what it embodies, is more mysterious, recalcitrant, surprising. (If only in detail, it's always, I think, at least *different.*)

What I've been arguing applies not only to long poems, but, as Coleridge suggests, to lyric. Kenneth Burke has a great essay called "Symbolic Action in a Poem by Keats."

Halliday: In your own work, have you found the "action" of a poem turning out to be significantly different from what you thought it would be, when you began the poem?

Bidart: I've just been through hell with a long poem in my third book, "Confessional." Six years ago, in the summer of 1976, I wrote the first part of the poem. I felt immediately that it wasn't complete, and wanted to write what I thought of as the second "half." And I knew what the last two lines of this second half must be. But that's all that I had that was specific, that was concrete.

Well, it took me six years to discover what the second half must be. That was a time of immense frustration—I would have loved to consider the first part (which was four pages) "complete." But my friends kept telling me it wasn't finished, and of course *I* knew it wasn't finished, that from the beginning I had felt there must be more (though I tried to repress the memory of feeling this). I had an arc in my head, a sense—frustratingly without content—of the shape of the emotional journey that had to take place, and (because I had the last two lines) the words on which it would end. That was all!

The poem is about my relationship to my mother, though it begins with an anecdote about a cat that *didn't* happen to me (it's from the memoirs of Augustus Hare). I felt, for complicated and opaque reasons, that this story was right at the beginning—that I needed it. Everything else in the poem had to be "true."

Slowly during those six years the second part grew in me. I say "grew" (and it *did* feel that way), but the process wasn't at all orderly or continuous. I read, in Peter Brown's wonderful *Augustine of Hippo,* the scene in the *Confessions* between Augustine and his mother at the window at Ostia. I felt immediately some version of this scene—as an embodiment of everything that between my mother and me *didn't* happen—should be in the poem. But *how* this could happen wasn't at all clear.

There is an "Elegy" for my mother in my second book. As I went back to it, I felt more and more dissatisfied with it—when "Elegy" was written, right around my mother's death, it was as true as I could make it, but it no longer represented what I felt about our relationship, the way (after several years had passed) I now saw it. I had to be, if not "fair" (who can know that?), *fairer.*

So the second part of the poem finally got itself written out of the desire to tell the whole thing again from the ground up, finally to get it "right." This desire in the end came to me clothed as necessity: I felt I *owed* it to my mother. The poem is still angry, just as "Elegy" was angry, but there's much more in it—among other things, much more sense of my complicity in everything that happened between us. What started out as the "second half" ended up three times as long (and was written six years later).

All art, of course, is artifice: words in our mouths, or our minds, don't just "naturally" happen on paper with focus, shape, or force. If, in a poem, we feel we are listening to a voice speak the things that most passionately engage it, it is an illusion. But I think that Frost's statement is also true: "No tears in the writer, no tears in the reader."

Halliday: Can you say more about "artifice" in a poem? In your own poems?

Bidart: There's a remarkable passage in a letter by Keats that for me stands for how genuinely mysterious and paradoxical this subject is. So often people use terms like "open form" or "closed form," or "sincere" or "artificial," as sticks to beat each other over the head. In the letter, Keats says that he is giving up "Hyperion," because it is too "Miltonic" and "artful": "there were too many Miltonic inversions in it—Miltonic verse cannot be written but in an artful or rather artist's humour. I wish to give myself up to other sensations." Then he suggests an experiment—that his reader pick out some lines from the poem, and put an "x" next to "the false beauty proceeding from art" and a double line next to "the true voice of feeling." There's something terrifically winning about Keats' desire to separate mere "art" (which led to falseness) from what he calls (in a great, beguiling phrase) "the true voice of feeling." Part of his greatness as a poet comes from the way he imagined the poet's job as discovering truth—from his sense (in the "Chamber of Maiden-Thought" letter) that his poems must "explore" the "dark passages" we find ourselves in after we see "into the heart and nature of Man"; from his impatient self-criticism of his poems, throughout his career, demanding that they "make discoveries."

So he asks his reader to put an "x" next to "the false beauty proceeding from art," and a double line next to "the true voice of feeling." Then there is an amazing passage: "Upon my soul 'twas imagination I cannot make the distinction—Every now & then there is a Miltonic intonation—But I cannot make the division properly." In other words, the distinction—so clear in "imagination"—cannot actually be made. There *are* things that seem only artifice ("Every now & then there is a Miltonic intonation"), but the *division* between what proceeds from "art," and "the true voice of feeling," cannot clearly or consistently be made.

I think "the true voice of feeling" is a necessary and useful ideal.

So many poems seem *not* to be, at any point, "the true voice of feeling." We have to have the "imagination" of it. But in practice, I'm sure there is no one way—free verse or formal verse, striving for "originality" or "imitation"—for us to achieve it. It's certainly not the opposite of "art."

Halliday: That seems to lead us back to the question we began with —the discovery of the subject matter of your first book, and of your own prosody. At what point did that happen?

Bidart: I began graduate school in 1962, and the first poem that I've kept was written in 1965. Those were years of bewilderment, ferment, and misery. Why was I in graduate school? I wasn't at all sure. I thought I would like to teach; but I also felt that if I didn't become an artist I would die. By the time I graduated from Riverside, I'd ceased believing I must, or could, become a film director. Rather murkily I felt that if I really *were* a film maker I would have already, somehow, in however a rudimentary a way, made a film. (I had shot a few feet, but they seemed stupid, arty, clumsy—and in any case, I couldn't connect them to a whole.) I felt the fact that this art could only be practiced if you convinced someone else to risk huge sums of money, the fact that movies were a business, would break me; Antonioni had said he spent ten years waiting in producers' waiting rooms before he was allowed to direct a film.

So I went to graduate school at Harvard—more out of the desire to continue the world of conversations and concerns I had found in an English Department as an undergraduate, than out of any clear conviction about why I was there. I took courses with half my will—often finishing the work for them months after they were over; and was scared, miserable, hopeful. I wrote a great deal. I wrote lugubrious plays that I couldn't see had characters with no character. More and more, I wrote poems.

I began this interview by saying that discovering the subject matter of *Golden State,* as the *necessary* subject matter for me at that time, was bound up with discovering a prosody. This seems to me true; but I'm nervous that describing this process as a narrative, consecutive and chronological, will introduce far more order into it than existed. It was a time of terrible thrashing around.

So let me describe this period in terms of "problems." First, I felt how literary, how "wanting to be like other writers"—particularly like the modernists, and "post-modernists"—the animating impulses behind my poems were. I said to myself (I remember this very clearly): "If what fills your attention are the great works that have been written—*Four Quartets* and *Ulysses* and 'The Tower' and *Life Studies* and *Howl* (yes, *Howl*) and *The Cantos*—nothing is *left* to be done. You couldn't possibly make anything as inventive or sophisticated or complex. But if you turn from them, and what you look at is your *life*: NOTHING is figured out; NOTHING is understood. . . . *Ulysses* doesn't describe your life. It doesn't teach you how to lead your life. You don't know what *love* is; or *hate*; or *birth*; or *death*; or *good*; or *evil*. If what you look at is your *life,* EVERYTHING remains to be figured out, ordered; EVERYTHING remains to be done. . . ."

However silly this speech may sound, "recollected in tranquillity," it was a kind of turning-point for me. I realized that "subject matter"—confronting the dilemmas, issues, "things" with which the world had confronted me—had to be at the center of my poems if they were to have force. If a poem is "the mind in action," I had to learn how to *use* the materials of a poem to *think*. I said to myself that my poems must seem to embody not merely "thought," but *necessary* thought. And necessary thought (rather than mere rumination, ratiocination) expresses or acknowledges what has resisted thought, what has forced or irritated it into being.

Such an aim has huge implications, of course, for *prosody*—versification, how words are linked and deployed on the page. I needed a way to get "the world" onto the page (bits of dialogue, scenes, other voices, "facts"), as well as the mind *acting* on, ordering, resisting it. This sounds like the way that I earlier described *The Cantos* —how Pound managed to create a texture which seemed to allow *anything* into the poem without changing its identity. Pound does this, predominately, by using the "ideogram," the "ideogrammic method": by placing image next to image, quotation next to quotation, bit of cultural artifact next to bit of cultural artifact, allowing "meaning" to arise from the juxtapositions. The result is that the page often feels essentially static (though also often giving a sense of "sudden illumination" or "sudden liberation"). This static (though luminous) texture just did not feel like my experience of the mind, the way the mind acts upon and within the world. I needed a way to embody the mind moving *through* the elements of its world, actively contending with and organizing them, while they somehow retain the illusion of their independence and nature, are felt as "out there" or "other."

Slowly I stumbled toward "deploying" the words on the page through voice; syntax; punctuation. (By "punctuation" I mean not merely commas, periods, etc., but line breaks, stanza breaks, capital letters—all the ways that speed and tension and emphasis can be marked.)

Halliday: I've heard you talk, many times, about "voice" and "punctuation" in your work, but not "syntax." How is it connected in your mind with the others?

Bidart: Syntax—the ways words are linked to make phrases, phrases to make sentences, even sentences to make "paragraphs"—has had a huge effect on the punctuation of my poems. Often the syntax is extremely elaborate. As the voice moves through what it is talking about—trying to lay out, acknowledge, organize the "material"—it needs dependent clauses, interjections, unfinished phrases, sometimes whole sentences in apposition. The only way I can sufficiently *articulate* this movement, express the relative weight and importance of the parts of the sentence—so that the reader knows where he or she is and the "weight" the speaker is placing on the various elements that are being laid out—is punctuation. In "Confessional," in the section based on Augustine, whole typed pages are single sentences (the sentences are longer than Augustine's own). Punctuation allows me to "lay out" the *bones* of a sentence visually, spatially, so that the reader can see the pauses, emphases, urgencies and languors in the voice.

The punctuation of my poems has become increasingly elaborate; I'm ambivalent about this. I feel I've been forced into it—*without* the heavy punctuation, again and again I seemed not to be able to get the movement and voice "right." The Nijinsky poem was a nightmare. There is a passage early in it that I got stuck on, and didn't solve for two years. Undoubtedly there were a number of reasons for this; the poem scared me. Both the fact that I thought it was the best thing I had done, and Nijinsky's ferocity, the extent to which his mind is *radical,* scared me. But the problem was also that the movement of his voice is so mercurial, and paradoxical: many simple declarative sentences, then a long, self-loathing, twisted-against-itself sentence. The *volume* of the voice (from very quiet to extremely loud) was new; I found that many words and phrases had to be not only entirely capitalized, but in italics.

Discovering punctuation that you haven't used before, because you need it, is *hard.* Probably the crucial instance of this, for me, was in "Golden State" (the poem). The phrase I couldn't get right is in the eighth section: "The exacerbation/ of this seeming *necessity/* for connection". The problem was the punctuation following "connection." The entire phrase (three lines long) comes as a kind of pained distillate or residue of everything above it on the page; it must seem itself both a *result*, and blocked; the next lines are about what in reality preceded it, what is "beneath" it both on the page and as cause. I punctuated the lines differently for months, to the point where my friends winced when I pulled out a new version. The solution I finally found is "double-punctuation": a dash followed by a semicolon. Coming to it was so hard that I felt I had discovered this mark, this notation, all by myself. Later I found it in poems I had known very well—in "Grandparents" from *Life Studies,* for example. But because I hadn't understood it before, understood its necessity, I'd never seen it. (Finding the capitalized "MYSELF" in "Herbert White" was also a long drama—I couldn't get the word right until I saw a capitalized "MOI" in Valéry's "La Jeune Parque.")

James has a wonderful phrase: "the thrilling ups and downs of the compositional problem."

Halliday: And now your third term—"voice."

Bidart: Surely the logic—or self-serving calculation—of everything I've said is now clear. The nature of the syntax and punctuation has to proceed from the demands, the nature, of the voice. (In the "Genesis" translation, for example—where whatever speaks the poem couldn't be more different from the voices usually in my poems—the punctuation is quite spare and simple, except for capitalization.)

A little more history is relevant here. The teacher I was closest to at Riverside was Tom Edwards—he is a great teacher. His sophomore survey course, "The English Literary Tradition," was the place that I feel I first learned how to pay attention to the details of a poem, to how it is made. The importance of "voice" and "tone of voice" was at the heart of what I learned. Edwards' teacher had been Reuben Brower, and Brower's teacher (or almost-teacher) at Amherst was Frost. "Tone of voice" and "speaker" were crucial terms for Brower, and of course for Frost. Frost has the great statement about "voice":

> A dramatic necessity goes deep into the nature of the sentence. Sentences are not different enough to hold the attention unless they are dramatic. No ingenuity of varying structure will do. All that can save them is the speaking tone of voice somehow entangled in the words and fastened to the page for the ear of the imagination. That is all that can save poetry from sing-song, all that can save prose from itself.

I only read those sentences in graduate school, but I had absorbed them (or been absorbed by them), through Edwards, just at the time I was first seriously studying poetry. For Frost, this emphasis on "the speaking tone of voice" isn't separate from the importance of meter: "The possibilities for tune from the dramatic tones of meaning struck across the rigidity of a limited meter are endless." In Frost's terms, my poems—which rely so nakedly on voice, where everything in the prosody is in the service of the voice—just are "playing tennis without the net."

But he acknowledges how mysterious and peculiar these questions are: "the speaking tone of voice *somehow* entangled in the words and fastened to the page for the ear of the imagination." My work has been a long odyssey struggling to find ways to accomplish this "entangling" and "fastening"—a journey which starts in my own "ear of the imagination," and hopes to end there in the reader.

When I write, I always hear a "voice" in my head; and I always write in lines. I've never written a poem first as prose and then broken it into lines. The voice only embodies itself in words as the words break themselves in lines. (This movement is felt physically, in my body.) "Syntax" is dependent on this; the sentence can only take on a certain shape, have a certain syntax, as the voice finds that the sentence can be extended—can take on "new materials," and shape itself—across the lines.

But I find that *at the most intense moments* the line breaks are often not quite right. And the punctuation of the poem, including spaces between stanzas, initially is never right. The final punctuation is *not* an attempt to make the poem look the way I read it aloud; rather, the way I read it aloud tries to reproduce what I hear in my head. But once I finally get the typed page to the point where it does seem "right"—where it does seem to reproduce the voice I hear —something very odd happens: the *"being"* of the poem suddenly becomes the poem on paper, and no longer the "voice" in my head. The poem on paper suddenly seems a truer embodiment of the poem's voice than what I still hear in my head. I've learned to trust this when it happens—at that point, the entire process is finished.

Halliday: How does what you've said about prosody connect with the "subject matter" of *Golden State*?

Bidart: When I first faced the central importance of "subject matter," I knew what I would have to begin by writing about. In the baldest terms, I was someone who had grown up obsessed with his parents. The drama of their lives dominated what, at the deepest level, *I* thought about. Contending with them (and with the worlds of Bakersfield and Bishop, California, where I had grown up) was how I had learned—in the words of Bruno Walter about Bruckner and Mahler, which I quote in "Golden State"—to "think my life."

The great model for such poems was of course *Life Studies.* I had read it soon after it came out, and like so many others was knocked over. But I knew that Lowell's experience of the world he came from, and himself as an actor in it, was very different from *my* experience. Lowell's poems were written when he was around forty, and seemed to me to communicate an overwhelmingly grim, helpless sense that the dragons in his life were simply *like that.* At seven, he was "bristling and manic"—without any sense of *cause*. "Tamed by *Miltown*, we lie on Mother's bed;/ the rising sun in war paint dyes us red": these poems are great glowing static panels in brilliant super-saturated technicolor, a world that refuses knowledge of the *causes* beneath it, without chance for change or escape.

But I was twenty-six, not forty—and *my* poems had to be about trying to figure out *why* the past was as it was, what patterns and powers kept me at its mercy (so I could change, and escape). The prosody of my poems could *not* reflect the eloquent, brilliantly concrete world of *Life Studies*; it had to express a drama of processes, my attempts to organize and order, and failures to organize and order. It had to dramatize the moments when I felt I had *learned* the terrible wisdom of the past (so I could unlearn it).

So rather than trying to replicate *Life Studies,* I was engaged in an argument with it. If *Life Studies* had done what I felt my poems had to do, I'm sure I couldn't have written them. Later, when I met Lowell—in 1966, after I'd written "California Plush" but before "Golden State"—I found that he shared this conscious sense of being engaged in an *argument* with the past. He liked to quote Edward Young: "He who imitates the *Iliad* does not imitate Homer."

Halliday: So he was not your teacher, then, in the sense of being the central guiding voice in your mind as you built that book.

Bidart: I didn't learn a prosody from him; and I certainly didn't want to write the poems he had already written. I somehow always knew that "what I had to say" was different from what he was saying; that's why, I think, though I got tremendously close to him and his work in later years, I never felt that as an artist I was about to be annihilated.

But much before I met him, I had known his work extremely well—I had admired it, and learned from it, in the way that I admired and learned from Eliot and Pound. And later, I sat and listened to him in class, for years; it would be impossible to listen to a mind that various and inventive and surprising and learned and iconoclastic and craftsmanlike, *without* learning things. The fact that later I could be useful, both as a reader of his poems and a friend, to someone I so much revered, was a profound event in my life: a *healing* event. I saw him in every kind of vicissitude, from insanity to suffering gratuitous humiliations; he *grew* in my eyes, the more intimately I knew him.

Halliday: When did you begin to write dramatic monologues?

Bidart: "Herbert White" begins *Golden State,* and was written at the same time as the family poems. I wanted to make a Yeatsian "anti-self"—someone who was "all that I was not," whose way of "solving problems" was the *opposite* of that of the son in the middle of the book. The son's way (as I have said) involves trying to "analyze" and "order" the past, in order to reach "insight"; Herbert White's is to give himself to a violent pattern growing out of the dramas of his past, a pattern that consoles him as long as he can feel that someone *else* has acted within it. I imagined him as a voice coming from a circle in Hell. The fact that he is an "anti-self" only has some meaning, I thought, if he *shares* something fundamental with me; I gave him a family history related to my own. He has another embodiment at the end of the book: the "MONSTER" who can only face his nature if he "splits apart," and who asks the "I" of the poem to help him to do so. I put "Herbert White" at the beginning because I felt the book had to begin "at the bottom"—in the mind of someone for whom the issues in the book were in the deepest disorder. He is the chaos everything else in the book struggles to get out of.

So "Herbert White" wasn't an escape from the world of the family poems—but I think the dramatic monologues I've written since are. *Golden State* did in fact do for me what I wanted it to do; I felt I had been able to "get all the parts of the problem" out there. I've never had to write about my father or Bakersfield again. (Will I?) It seemed to settle those issues for me. It drained those subjects of their obsessive power.

I think that it did this *because* I was able to "get all the parts of the problem" out there. My mother isn't at the center of *Golden State,* and as I've said, the poem about her in my second book didn't seem to me deep enough or true enough. I hope "Confessional" completes something.

Halliday: Can you say more about the dramatic monologues you've written since "Herbert White"? Are the concerns beneath them as "personal"?

Bidart: I've never been able to get past Yeats' statement that out of our argument with others we make rhetoric, out of our argument with ourselves we make poetry. At times that's seemed to me the profoundest thing ever said about poetry.

Williams said, "No ideas but in things"—but by that he *didn't* mean "no ideas." His work is full of ideas, full of "arguments with himself." By the end of another poem he manages to convince us that "The pure products of America/ go crazy" (an idea), as well as that this most American of writers is riven to say it. The drive to conceptualize, to *understand* our lives, is as fundamental and inevitable as any other need. So a poem must include it, make it part of its "action." The ideas that are articulated in the course of the action don't "solve" or eradicate or end it, if the drama is true enough or important enough, any more than they do in the action of our lives.

So the dramatic monologues I've written since *Golden State,* insofar as they are animated by "arguments with myself," don't seem to me any less (or more) "personal." The books have been animated by issues: issues revolving around the "mind-body" relation in *The Book of the Body*; "guilt" (and ramifications) in *The Sacrifice.* No genuine issue, in my experience, has an "answer" or "solution." But the argument within oneself about them is still inevitable and necessary. In "Ellen West" and the Nijinsky poem, I didn't feel I was "making up" the voice or "making up" the drama —they were *there,* and I felt that to write the poems I had to let them (both the *voices* and the *issues* their lives embody the torments and dilemmas of) enter me. Of course they were already inside me (though I still had to let them in).

The most intense version of this that I've ever experienced happened with the Nijinsky poem. It was written in about a month, and during that month there was an independent voice in my head that insistently had things to say. I knew that I was, in effect, feeding it things, feeding it things I had thought about; but the voice had an identity and presence in my head that seemed independent of my conscious mind, and I was not simply telling it when to talk and when not to talk. On the contrary, the minute I would finish a section, the voice would begin making up new sentences and obsessing about the next stage of the drama. And one reason I felt certain that the poem *was* finished when it was finished, that the "action" was completed, was that at the end of the poem the voice just disappeared. The voice had no more to say: when I wrote the last line of the poem, the voice just ceased.

Halliday: At the beginning of this interview, you said something enigmatic about "the struggle to make life *show* itself in a work of art."

Bidart: There is a scene in "Herbert White" in which he is looking out the window of his room at home, and feels suffocated by the fact that everything is "just *there,* just *there,* doing nothing!/ not saying anything!" He wants to see beneath the skin of the street, to see (in Wordsworth's terms) "into the life of things," and cannot. It's of course me feeling that. So much of our ordinary lives seems to refuse us—seems almost dedicated to denying us—knowledge of what is beneath the relatively unexceptional surface of repeated social and economic relations.

The artist's problem is to make life *show* itself. Homer, Aeschylus, Vergil, Shakespeare—a great deal of Western art has made life *show* itself by dramatizing crisis and disaster. Lear, in his speech about "pomp," says that when he was king he saw nothing. Success, good fortune, power cut him off from seeing into the nature of things. Out of his blindness and vanity, he performs the stupid act that precipitates his "fall." But when he *does* "fall," he sees much more than simply his former blindness, his stupidity. He can't stop from falling—from discovering our ineradicable poverty, and defying the heavens to "change or cease." In the course of the play, Lear "learns" things, but the play couldn't exactly be called the story of his education: Cordelia dies, and he dies.

When Lear "falls," the forces that before were present—but dormant, unseen, unacknowledged—then manifest themselves. (Only then.)

Many other works of art of course *are* "the story of an education." Wordsworth's "spots of time" and Joyce's "epiphanies" were moments they eagerly hoarded and clung to—for these moments seemed to them moments of true insight, with emblematic force, the story of the true education of their souls. They embedded these moments in narrative contexts, in actions, dramatizing their *access* to them.

Again and again, insight is dramatized by showing the conflict between what is ordinarily seen, ordinarily understood, and what now is experienced as real. Cracking the shell of the world; or finding that the shell is cracking under you.

The unrealizable ideal is to write as if the earth opened and spoke. I think that if the earth *did* speak, she would espouse no one set of values, affections, meanings, that everything embraced would also somehow be annihilated and denied.

Notes

"The War of Vaslav Nijinsky" (page 21)
Readers not familiar with Nijinsky's life may find some biographical background useful. Nijinsky came to the West as the principal male dancer of the Ballets Russes—which was directed by the man who had created it, Serge Diaghilev. He lived with Diaghilev for several years. With Diaghilev's encouragement, he became a choreographer: he did the first productions of, among others, "L'Après-midi d'un Faune" (1912), "Le Sacre du Printemps" (1913). Revolutionary, modernist, his choreography remained as controversial as his dancing was admired. On the company's first trip to South America —Diaghilev, who hated sea travel, was absent—Nijinsky met and married a young woman traveling with the troupe, Romola de Pulszky. The break with Diaghilev precipitated by this was never healed.

Prose passages in the poem are based on Romola Nijinsky's biography, *Nijinsky* (Simon and Schuster, 1934), and sentences by Richard Buckle, Serge Lifar, Maurice Sandoz.

"Two Men" (page 10)
These lines are indebted to an unpublished lecture by V. A. Kolve, "Fools In and Out of Motley" (Wellesley College, 1979).

"The Book of the Body" (page 106)
Lines 12–15: Vergil, *Eclogue V*, 56–57.

"Ellen West" (page 109)
This poem is based on Ludwig Binswanger's "Der Fall Ellen West," translated by Werner M. Mendel and Joseph Lyons (*Existence*, Basic Books, 1958). Binswanger names his patient "Ellen West."

"After Catullus" (page 169)
Catullus, *Carmen LVI* ("O rem ridiculam, Cato, et iocosam").

"The First Hour of the Night" (page 183)
The source for the "dream of the history of philosophy," and the major source for the poem as a whole, is Wilhelm Dilthey's "The Dream," translated by William Kluback (*The Philosophy of History in Our Time*, Doubleday/Anchor Books, 1959). The final dream is based on a dream reported by E. L. Grant Watson in a letter to Jung (C. G. Jung, *Letters*, Vol. 2, p. 146, note 1; Princeton University Press, 1975).

(There is a space between stanzas at the bottom of each page of verse, except on pages 109, 111, 146, 167.)